Dominican Spirituality

Dominican Spirituality

An Exploration

Erik Borgman

Translated by John Bowden

CONTINUUM

London and New York

Continuum
The Tower Building, 11 York Road, London SE1 7NX
370 Lexington Avenue, New York, NY 10017-6503

ISBN 0 8264 5684 7

Acknowledgment
The article 'Dominican Spirituality' by Edward Schillebeeckx, translated by
John Bowden, originally appeared in *God among Us; The Gospel Proclaimed*,
SCM Press 1983, pp. 232-48, and is reproduced here by kind permission.

Printed and bound in Great Britain by
Creative Print and Design, Wales

Contents

Foreword

Timothy Radcliffe OP

This book is a highly attractive and stimulating exposition of Dominican spirituality by Erik Borgman, a Dutch Lay Dominican. The central intuition of the book is that Dominican spirituality is founded on the encounter of God in all of human experience. Dominic's experience in the early thirteenth century was born in opposition to Catharism, which maintained that God was remote from us and that there was a fundamental opposition between the divine and this material world. But for Dominic it is here, in our lives, with all their creativity and goodness, their mess and confusion, that God is to be found. Our mission as preachers pushes us 'to enter the unrest of the street and the inn, politics and journalism, welfare, teaching and science, in the belief that the holy, the traces of the Holy One, are to be found there' (p.28). Even in the most difficult situations, when all is dark, God is waiting to be discovered. 'If Dominican spirituality has a core, then it would be this insight into the unexpected and unheard-of nearness of God' (p.38). This is the good news that the Order of Preachers was founded to preach and the source of the happiness of the preacher.

This belief that God is there in our lives waiting to be discovered is fundamental to Erik Borgman's most attractive presentation of the Dominican tradition of prayer and contemplation. Contemplation is not the discovery of God through retreat from the world, though sometimes we need such moments. It is opening our eyes to discover God waiting for us in the most unpromising situations. The discipline of the contemplative life liberates us from the banal and trivial way of looking at things and at each other which is characteristic of the world of consumerism. We learn to see properly, to see in the dark, and above all to see compassionately, as God sees us. The contemplative must dare to be vulnerable to the pain and suffering of this world and 'to allow ourselves to be touched by what happens to us and the world around, in the belief that in this way we come upon the traces of the God of salvation and liberation' (p.40).

This contemplative gaze is also the fruit of study and reflection, of acquiring a 'thinking heart', in the words of the Jewish writer Etty Hillesum, who died in Auschwitz in 1943. Borgman's under-standing of Dominican spirituality is summed up in the superb image of a radio antenna, which broadcasts what it receives. Dominican spirituality, he maintains, is a matter of developing that receptivity to the presence of God which is the source of all our preaching.

Given the fundamental emphasis that Borgman places on finding the traces of God in our contemporary lives, it is not surprising that his interpretation of Dominican spirituality is strongly marked by the context in which he writes, that of the Dutch Church today. In Holland, religious life, in the classic sense, is undergoing a greater crisis than anywhere else in the world. The most flourishing branch of the Order is that of the Lay Dominicans, which is enjoying a marvellous renaissance This is reflected in his view that Dominican spirituality finds its pre-eminent expression in the life of lay people. In most parts of the world, all the branches of the Order – the friars, nuns and sisters – are blessed with vocations and vitality, which might lead one to stress other aspects of our spirituality. But it is also part of Dominican spirituality to delight in discovering that we do not always agree, as Borgman disagrees with me in one chapter of this book. Argument in the pursuit of truth is part of our Dominican life. He writes that 'being a true Dominican consists first and foremost in becoming part of the company of seekers and questioners, so as in this way, with the help of human reason and building on the Christian tradition, to find something of an answer' (p.28).

This excellent little book is enriched by the addition of a beautiful and packed article on Dominican spirituality by the Flemish friar, Edward Schillebeeckx OP, which brings out the fundamental tension at its centre, the dialogue between Christian tradition and the gospel on the one hand and the present moment, with its questions and insights, on the other. Like Borgman,

Schillebeeckx emphasizes the flexibility of Dominican life, in its response to the contemporary world, 'the grace to understand this century', as Lacordaire wrote. It is an itinerant and pilgrim spirituality. Schillebeeckx also underlines the absolutely priority of God's grace in all that we do, which is the basis of our trust in God, and that joy which is central to Dominican life, giving us 'a tranquil and happy spirituality'. The title of one of Schillebeeckx's latest books, *I am a Happy Theologian*, sums up well much of what it means to be a Dominican.

Introduction: Life Today as Religious Life: The renewed importance of a tradition

In the second half of the nineteenth century, when the majority of the Indians in the United States had been exterminated and the survivors had been banished to reservations, with neither power nor influence, their way of life was discovered by Americans of European origin. This life, so close to nature, seemed to be an attractive alternative to the urbanization, the industrialization and the consumer society which were beginning to come into being.

It sometimes seems that the same sort of thing is happening through the present-day interest in religion and spirituality. In this connection, interest in the religious life is particularly remarkable.

The religious life: a museum piece?

Though those who live in monasteries and convents are growing older and older, and in the Netherlands many orders and congregations see the end in sight, at the same time there is great interest in their way of life. When the monasteries, convents and priories in the Netherlands held open house for anyone who wanted to pay a visit on a day in the spring of 2000, the interest was overwhelming. And the guest rooms in monasteries are attracting more and more visitors. In an extrovert culture, many people are making contact with the world of the religious because they have the feeling that in it the inner life still has a central place. Men and women who find themselves being dragged along by the rapid pace of life are temporarily seeking in a monastery or convent an order which makes it possible for them to experience time as a form of eternity.

This clearly does people good. But at the same time it seems that for many men and women today the cloistered religious life is attractive precisely because it bears little relation to the life that they otherwise live. To exaggerate the point: much present-day interest in the religious life seems to derive from an amazement that a form of life which has become impossible in our cultural climate nevertheless still exists. Because of the effort required by everyday life, because of the burden of having to be increasingly emancipated and well informed in order to be successful in social and personal life, people in our time need places which offer tranquillity and space, places where they are temporarily relieved of their many duties. They long for a life which is not orientated on domination and control, but on receptiveness and openness to whatever offers itself. And they evidently find something of this life in monasteries and religious communities.

However, only a few actually think of sharing permanently in the life of the community of which they are guests. The enclosed communal religious life in the form which came into being above all in the nineteenth century, and of which we seem to be experiencing the declining days, is an oasis of calm for a notably large number of people, but it is evidently no real alternative to their demanding existence. However much they may enjoy taking part in it for a while, for them the cloistered form of religious life is not a real option. It is very worthwhile for there to be places where people can know that they are temporarily relieved of the responsibility of standing up for themselves and those with whom they are associated, places where they can feel that life cannot and must not be organized, but where they know that they are cherished and supported at the deepest level 'for nothing'. But it does seem problematical that interest in the religious life is thus comparable to an interest in old houses or conservation areas in towns and villages. Here people talk of 'museum pieces'. Old objects in a museum, old listed buildings, customs from folklore no longer form part of real life, and it is precisely that which makes them attractive. They give people the possibility of taking time off from the everyday obligation to be alert to the latest novelty on offer. Alongside the hectic instability of everyday life, they suggest a continuity and stability in which people can cherish themselves for a while.

Life today as religious life

If this is how the religious life appears to men and women today, then one of its most important characteristics could be left out. At the best moments of their history, the forms of religious life that have been devised make it clear that this life is really possible. The most important characteristic of religious life is that it can be realized. It is a practical possibility for men and women of flesh and blood, for those of us who are fully children of our own time, with all the questions and possibilities, fears and sensitivities that this involves, to lead a truly religious existence. That means an existence bound up with, devoted to, orientated on the holy and the Holy One. Such an existence is possible, and can be realized.

If this book is about religious life, it is about such a life: a life that can be realized and lived out, dedicated and wholesome. It is a life based on dedication to the holy, and along this way on dedication to the God of salvation who is spoken of in the Jewish and Christian traditions as the God of promise, of liberation, of righteousness, of healing and reconciliation. So here religious life is not presented as being fundamentally different from the life which people normally lead in our time. Religious life is not the opposite of the life that our culture has in store for us; it is not a life which is miraculously full of what is painfully lacking elsewhere. Here our own time is not depicted as a wilderness of godforsakenness in which the religious life can then be an oasis. This book points in the opposite direction. It seeks to break with the presupposition that in religious terms contemporary life is a wilderness. The religious life is about living and experiencing one's contemporary situation as a religious situation. It is not as if our time primarily *needs* religion and spirituality. There is no gap in our souls – for example the need to give depth to our lives – nor is there a gap in our society – for example the need for a foundation for values and norms – which the Christian tradition, Christian spirituality and the tradition of the religious life are to fill. Like any time, ours too is a religious time. This emerges at present particularly from the way in which after a long period of secularization religion is again very much the focal point of interest.

Thus it becomes clear that from a particular perspective our questions about existence are religious questions and the answers to them, the ways of dealing with them which we find, are religious answers and religious forms. So our life already *is* a religious life. Perhaps the religion that takes shape in it is a false religion; perhaps the form that life assumes is a perverse form. At any rate, that remains to be seen. But the life of men and women in our time is in any case already a religious life. They trust what they feel to be trustworthy, and they devote themselves to and work for what is holy to them. And they allow themselves to be guided by what they regard as a sustaining power, which perhaps is ultimately divine.

The aim of this book

According to some people the tradition of the religious life is completely out of date. According to others this tradition is important because it maintains what is forgotten elsewhere. My starting point is that the tradition of the religious life is not alien to what men and women today are striving for and seeking, but can give a new colour to this effort and this quest. My aim is to show clearly that the tradition of the religious life in general and the Dominican tradition in particular is capable of shedding light on the questions of men and women today and suggesting a way of dealing with them. These questions are ultimately a variant of the one central question of human existence, bound up with a particular time, place and person: the question of a good and meaningful life. The traditions of religious life do not give a direct answer to this question; rather, they are focused on keeping it permanently open. If that becomes clear once again, these traditions can help people – at any rate they help me – to find their own form of religious life, by giving conscious form to their existence as an existence that is dedicated to what seems to them to be good and holy, an existence that is a trace of the one who is Good and Holy *par excellence*.

With this in view, in the chapters which follow I have tried to look frankly at the traditions of the religious life, especially at the Dominican tradition. Here my starting point is the basic conviction that a religious and dedicated life cannot be lived anywhere else than in the midst of our turbulent culture, which constantly makes us uncertain. In other words, this book is deliberately written from the perspective of someone who in ecclesiastical jargon is called a 'lay person'. As will become clear, this has consequences for the interpretation of the Dominican tradition and for what is deemed to be important in it. However, this perspective has consequences not only for the content but also for the structure of my book. Most introductions to a tradition of religious life begin with its origins, describe the aims of the founder, follow the later history and end up with its contemporary forms. This book begins at the other end. In the different chapters I constantly look for the present-day forms of the questions which lie at the basis of the religious life. Then I explore what light falls on these questions from the Dominican tradition of the religious life. The key question is how a life which without qualification is involved in the contemporary situation can be seen as religious life. And I discuss the Dominican past to the degree that this sheds some light here.

So the structure of this book is not historical but thematic. The first chapter discusses what religious life is, and the second investigates the distinctive Dominican perspective on religious life. The third chapter speaks about the specifically Dominican relationship between seeing the holy and being dedicated to the holy – in Dominican jargon, between contemplation and action. The fourth chapter deals with prayer in the Dominican sense and the fifth with an itinerant existence as the specifically Dominican form of life. The great figures from Dominican history – like Dominic, Catherine of Siena, Thomas Aquinas, Bartholomé de Las Casas and Francisco de Vitoria – and the less great will be discussed within this framework, sometimes at considerable length. However, the approach here will not be primarily historical, as to people from a distant past. These figures will be portrayed as our spiritual ancestors. In their own way and in their own time they wrestled with questions which now concern us and therefore it makes sense to get to know their thoughts and views. It is not that once and for all they formulated the right answer to these questions, or even the definitive Dominican answer. But if in our consideration of our situation we learn from the way in which they dealt with theirs, if we make use of what they thought about questions which concern us, an insight is revealed which is really ours, which looks specifically at our situation, but at the same time is in line with the Dominican tradition. Where this happens, we continue the Dominican tradition.

So the chapters of *Dominican Spirituality. An Exploration* have not been written as if there were a Dominican tradition which needs only to be expounded to men and women of our time for it to be capable of becoming fruitful again. All the chapters are intended as explorations of our own situation and the Dominican tradition in the light of each other. In this way, if it succeeds, a new truth will slowly become visible.

Refounding Dominican life

Those who see the Dominican tradition as a clarification of their own situation and the situation today apparently think that this tradition can be continued only by being radically renewed. From the 1960s on, this conviction has led religious to experiment practically with new forms of religious life and to reflect on them theologically. Such experiments, usually on a small scale, have taken place in Dominican circles and are still going on. It is thanks to those who have embarked on them that it is possible at all to write differently about the religious life, as I do in this book.

These people have made it clear that anyone who wants to continue the Dominican tradition of religious life at the beginning of the twenty-first century faces the same task as the French Dominican Henri-Dominique Lacordaire around 1840. In the 1820s, 1830s and 1840s Lacordaire became convinced that Catholicism needed to adopt a completely new form after the French Revolution. It needed to find its place again in a democracy in which the church no longer played a central role in public life through the person of the king. Lacordaire found points of contact in the Dominican tradition for the renewal which he felt necessary. So he refounded the Dominican Order in France; like other religious orders it had been banned since the French Revolution. Lacordaire succeeded in having this ban lifted and re-establishing a Dominican province in France. He became one of the first members, and subsequently also its head. But he also refounded the Order in the sense that he re-read the Dominican past bearing in mind questions that were topical in his time. Out of the Dominican tradition he received insights which in his time had almost been forgotten in Dominican circles, and he also took initiatives that would give form to the Dominican life in a new way appropriate to his own time. I am convinced that we now face a similar task today.

While preparing for his definitive entry into the Dominican Order, Lacordaire wrote a book about Dominic. In it he was able to portray the founder of the Dominican Order in a way which was surprisingly topical for his time. While about twenty of us were busy preparing to enter the Dominican Lay Community of the Netherlands, which was finally refounded with the support of the Dutch Dominicans on 24 October 1999, the first chapters of the present book were being written. Texts were produced and commented on in a small group; then they were rewritten and finally read and discussed by more than twenty groups distributed over the Netherlands. Most of these groups noted down their comments and observations on the texts, and the various chapters emerged after a final revision on the basis of this commentary. I do not want to suggest that this book is in any way comparable in quality to Lacordaire's. But I have often had the feeling that our enterprise was akin to his: to depict the Dominican tradition in such a way that it proves meaningful for our own situation and is relevant to it.

Thus in a sense Lacordaire was our patron during the process of writing the book. But someone else was our mentor, without being aware of it. I would probably never even have had the idea of writing a book like this had I not seen another book of about the same length. In 1956, a year before I was born, the Dominican Michael Hensen wrote a little book called *Dominican Life in the World*. It was meant for members of what was then called the Dominican Third Order Community, a movement of individuals who were not religious and not priests, of women and men who lived in the world and tried to lead a Dominican life in their own way there: in their professional life and their domestic life, in their activities and their reflection. This Dutch section of the Dominican 'Third Order' is the forerunner of our Dominican Lay Community of the Netherlands. When I happened to read Hensen's book, in the midst of the antiquated words and ideas I came upon insights which I still found surprisingly topical. Among other things, Hensen wrote this:

> Don't you think that uncertainty is one of the most prominent characteristics of our time? Everyone feels that we are no longer travelling on a fixed compass bearing. We have been torn away from many familiar values. What our fathers and mothers still thought to be absolutely certain is at present in considerable doubt... Perhaps you are one of those people who are living spiritually in a kind of vacuum. Several old forms of faith no longer mean anything to you. You are looking for a new equilibrium, for more support, for a spiritual 'home' that meets your religious ideals. Now in our day there is a religious

movement that will help you in your idealism: the Dominican Third Order Community. This movement is not new. It has very old credentials. Its rule of life dates from 1285 and was laid down by the then Master of the Dominican Order, Munio de Zamora.`

I told a few Dominican friends about this. A number of us thought that it would be good if there could be a new book like Michael Hensen's, but now addressing the situation of almost 50 years later. So in 1998 Hans Beemer, Leny Beemer-de Vos, Els van der Ree and I began the process that I have just described. We wrote, discussed, rewrote, circulated the material and gathered the notes that were made about it. And not long afterwards we began with a rather larger group the process that was to result in the (re)founding of the Dominican Lay Community of the Netherlands, as it came to be called.

Those who link up with the Dominican Order here do so in the conviction that the Dominican tradition can take on new forms of expression, particularly in our situation, in which the resolute yet at the same time uncertain quest that Hensen already indicated in 1956 has become the form of religious commitment *par excellence*. This book derives from the same conviction and seeks to put this evocative power to the test. As a tribute to Hensen, the first versions of the chapters were disseminated under the title 'Dominican Life in the World Today'. However, this title seemed to us to be too dated, too little related to 'the world of today'.

It was largely due to Hans, Leny and Els that *Dominican Spirituality. An Exploration* actually came into being. Thanks are also due to all those who read these chapters and who now and then cautiously or boldly enquired when the rest that had been promised would appear – always later than intended or promised. In my view the text has been significantly improved by their observations, expressed with modesty or aplomb, which came to me in writing or by word of mouth.

No book about Dominican spirituality can be written without being rooted in the Dominican community and in Dominican groups, without conversation with Dominicans and contact with Dominican thinkers. At the same time, the text as I present it here is the account of my personal reflections on what I feel can be a credible spirituality, and of what in the Dominican tradition I have found to be of value. The result shows how I understand myself, in what sense I call myself a Dominican, and how I want to continue the Dominican tradition in an ongoing process of refounding. What I mean is that at the end of the day no one but me is responsible for the text. I do not present this book in the hope that others will imitate my views directly. I hope above all that it will prompt further discussion between people of different backgrounds, experiences and views.

Writing and reading as forms of prayer

In 1283 in Toulouse an anonymous Dominican wrote a book to instruct and support those who had just entered his Order. He prefaced his text with a prayer to the Holy Spirit that his words should be worthy of the divine message that he had to proclaim, although he himself as a person was unworthy of this message. In the Middle Ages it was customary to emphasize strongly one's own unworthiness as a messenger and thus bring out all the more sharply the exalted status of the message, but in our day there is something refreshing about such a relativizing of the role of the author. However, I find it moving that this Dominican writer observes that he knows that he is dependent on the prayer of the up-and-coming Dominicans for whom he is writing. In this way he shows that he realizes that his words cannot in themselves bring his readers into contact with God and cannot expound what true religious life is. Neither he nor what he says can bring about an encounter with what is holy and wholesome, and it is beyond his power to arrange an experience of traces of the divine Presence. His writers can really understand his concern only if they have already had such experiences elsewhere and are to have them again.

It will be clear that the texts in this book are not meant to be an introduction to the Dominican tradition like the text of this mediaeval novice-master from the south of France. But like him, I know that I am dependent on the readiness of readers to introduce their own experiences into the text and to read themselves out of it again. The words that I have written can perhaps point readers towards texts and images from the Dominican tradition or from contemporary literature which they do not yet know but which are nevertheless evocative. I hope that at particular moments the chapters which follow will set in motion a train of thought which awakens readers to what has hitherto been dormant, or provide a framework for what so far they have found difficult to give a place. But nothing in the following chapters can call anything to life. As a product of my own history and a view of what has taken place in it, everything that I write is dependent on what light has dawned in the history of readers – both individual and collective – in the past and what light may dawn in the future.

In other words, at the end of the day, writing and reading are forms of expectation and hope, forms of prayer.

1

In the Footsteps of Thecla: Dominican life as religious life for lay people

Life involves putting things in order. We have to find set times to do things and to arrange our affairs efficiently. How often do we go shopping, and where? What do we cook and how do we cook it? Who does the cooking? But life is also a matter of dividing things into 'my world' and 'not my world'. What do I buy and what do I eat, and what don't I eat? What won't I put on the table or can't I allow? With whom will I eat and for whom will I cook, and with and for whom will I certainly not? All kinds of arrangements like this make up who people are and how they see themselves. They define people's individual and collective identities.

So it is logical that many of the primal stories of humankind begin with the ordering of the world: with divisions and the significance of these divisions. What can be eaten and what cannot? What is high and what is low? Who has a say over what and over whom? What must be done when and by whom? But also: what must we do about the divisions which are an unavoidable part of our world? How must we understand the division between light and darkness, how do we deal with the difference between human beings and animals, how do we live with the distinction between male and female? How must we look at joy and prosperity, success and pleasure, and what are we to do with pain, suffering and death? Religious traditions are collections of words, gestures and images which are handed down because they have clarified such questions for people in the past. They connect human existence with what people imagine as the deepest foundation and the highest good.

Religious life in the broadest sense is living with these traditions, in the conviction that they can help us to find a place in our situation and in the world as a whole. Religious life is the attempt to take this tradition with the utmost seriousness, because this can help us to realize something of what we are 'in depth' or want 'finally' to be.

Religious life as a life that brings order

Thus religious life in the broad sense in which I want to talk about it in this book is primarily a practical matter. Theoretical reflections can help, but they are not decisive. This is also evident from the two most central texts about religious life in the history of Christianity in the West.

The first was written by Aurelius Augustine, probably in 397, for a group of men who wanted to begin to live together in order to lead a life that was really good. They planned to break with the world, with inequality and the quest for money and honour which was predominant in the world of their day as it is in ours, and which at the same time both spurred people on and loaded them down. Augustine did not try to argue that the life that he wanted to begin to lead with his friends was important and necessary. Nor did he try to prove that his proposal was in line with the biblical tradition. He certainly presupposed that it was, and he regularly quotes from the biblical writings, but for him the Bible is evidently not the foundation of the religious life. It may perhaps sound somewhat enigmatic, but in his eyes the basis of a community is the very desire to live as a community. Everything depends on the desire to be of one mind amidst all the rifts and divisions between people. For Augustine this unanimity is 'holy', and in his view dedication to it must always remain central. The desire for this supreme good is his own norm and itself makes clear what is to be done. What later came to be known as the 'Rule of Saint Augustine' is simply a provisional attempt to formulate what a life lived with this desire could look like.

Augustine begins his 'rule for the community', which was to have a tremendous influence in later history, as follows:

> The chief motivation for your sharing life together is to live harmoniously in the house and to have one heart and one soul seeking God (cf. Acts 4.32).

All the regulations which follow, about dealing with one another and with the rest of the world, serve to ensure that Augustine and his companions can really do what they want: live together in solidarity and unity, because such a life has a divine quality. 'Live then, all of you, in harmony and concord: honour God mutually in each other; you have become his temples.'

The desire for such a godly life is also the driving force for Benedict of Nursia. Shortly after 529 he wrote how in his view human existence can be organized as a school for such a life. As for Augustine, so too for Benedict the goal, the good life, is its own norm, which determines the establishment of the school and the material to be taught. It is simple and impossibly difficult at the same time. The rule of Benedict begins with the admonition, taken directly from Psalm 34 (vv.13-16, quoted in I Peter 3.10-11):

Who among you delights in life,
longs for time to enjoy prosperity?
Guard your tongue from evil,
your lips from any breath of deceit.
Turn from evil and do good,
seek peace and pursue it.

Thus in Benedict's view religious life is a life which is turned away from evil and towards the good, and is where peace is to be found. The impressive collection of rules and regulations which follow this text serve to make such a life indeed possible, to help people to be practical in turning away from evil, turning towards good, seeking and pursuing peace.

In short, religious life amounts to believing with the body. But the venerable status that the Rules of Augustine and Benedict have attained in the course of history can prove misleading and in fact are misleading. For many people these Rules suggest that the ordering of life which they describe is in itself good and exalted, that it is holy. This is reinforced by the fact that in the course of time people in the Catholic Church began to regard the religious life as a quite distinctive ordering of existence. The religious life came to mean distancing oneself from the world and the obligations which living and surviving in the world involve, and by this distancing being orientated on God. Religious life then appears to be a matter of fitting into an intrinsically holy order, which at most can change only in details. However, it seems historically more correct and spiritually more productive not to regard religious life as a life which has *been ordered* once and for all but as a life which *brings order*, a life *in search of order.* At any rate, that is the perspective in which it is discussed here.

Life as an open book

So in my view the religious life in the Dominican tradition ultimately proves to be a life which brings order, a life in search of order. A text has been handed down from the early history of the Dominican Order which indicates great differences in the lives of Dominicans in different regions and countries, deriving from the differences in their circumstances:

> Different countries have different customs, and from this diversity different people have introduced different things into the Order, although there is only one Order.

This is not without its problems. The person who points out these differences here, Jordan of Saxony, the highest superior – Master General – of the Dominicans from 1222 until his death in 1237, thinks that Dominican life must be regulated so that it is more uniform. Even in Dominican circles it is sometimes thought that the religious life is a life that corresponds to a fixed order. But Jordan, and the others who later made similar attempts in his footsteps, only succeeded to a very limited degree in making the Dominican life really uniform. That evidently goes too much against a basic Dominican intuition, though this was to be put into words only in the second half of the twentieth century. In a text which was added in 1969 to the texts which together set out to regulate Dominican life, it is said that Dominican presence must take shape time and again in a way which is appropriate to the time and the situation. But while this formulation may be recent in its approach, the attitude that is expressed in it is as old as Dominican history itself.

A central regulation in the rules which set out to order the Dominican life from the beginning is that any regulation can be changed if the circumstances make that necessary. In the religious life as Dominicans understand it, the important thing is to order existence in the most fruitful way within the given circumstances. In other words, the Dominican life is not an ordered life, but comes about by bringing order to life in one's own time and situation in such a way that a view arises of what is truly holy and authentically godly. Rather than requiring a fixed structure, this calls for forms which help people to be constantly alert, which increase their capacity to respond to specific questions and demands, to adapt to specific circumstances and possibilities. In the last chapter of this book I shall attempt to demonstrate at rather greater length that the regulations of the Dominican life are indeed orientated in this direction.

Roughly 50 years after the official foundation of the Dominicans as a religious order within the church in 1216, an Englishman who was one of them wrote about how admirable they were. He praised the symbolism of the official Dominican garb: a white habit with a black cloak. Black and white: he saw these as the colours of ink on paper, the colours of a written text. In this way he suggested that Dominican life needs to be like an open book which tells of an ordering that gives life a divine quality. The Dominican claim is evidently not that Dominican existence quite simply embodies the good, godly life, but that it tells of it and points towards it.

Dominicans indeed sometimes succeed here in the life that they lead and the work that they do. In so doing they live up to their calling. For Dominicans the important thing is not to follow existing rules but to find a way of ordering life which makes it possible to exist as an open book and equips one for doing so. The Dominican tradition can help in the quest to bring order in such a way. It offers words and images in which it is possible to reflect meaningfully on the desire for salvation and happiness. At its best moments it speaks a language which does not oppress and which makes it possible for the human desire for goodness and fellowship not to feel oppressive but supportive. Thus it helps towards finding a form of life in which one can experience and see that all that exists in the sphere of the divine presence.

According to official Catholic terminology, the religious life is *vita consecrata*. This is usually translated 'life dedicated to God' . The specific history of religious life in general and Dominican history in particular shows that in fact it is more a matter of 'dedicated life'. It is a life which points to and is dedicated to what comes to light as wholesome and holy. It is life in dependence on what offers itself as a trace of God's holiness.

Belonging to the seekers and questioners

If the Dominican life at its best moments is a book that talks about what is holy with reference to God, the Holy One, the best Dominican books are about leading such a life.

The first theological book to be written in Dutch, the *Tafel van den Kersten Ghelove* (Table of Christian Faith) by the Dominican Dirc van Delf, is not addressed to a public of professional theologians. When this book was written, around 1400, such people spoke, read and wrote Latin. Very little theology was done in the different vernaculars, for scholars were generally convinced that those who lived in the world in which these vernaculars were used in daily life had no need of it. For them, concrete instructions about how they should behave sufficed. For instance, *Der Leken Spieghel* (An Example for the Laity), written about 50 years earlier by Jan van Boendale, is a practical guide for a moral and respectable life. It is therefore striking that in his *Tafel van den Kersten Ghelove* Dirc van Delf went into theological questions at some length. In my view this is a typically Dominican trait of Master Dirc.

Dirc van Delf does not limit himself to telling his readers what the church requires them to believe and what they have to do if they want to go through life as respectable Christians. He wants to give them insight. He makes use of all kinds of stories of different origin to bring the subject-matter close to their daily experience and adapts it to their daily concerns and problems by adding practical conclusions to his observations. However, for Dirc van Delf, reflection on what is deepest in life and what finally makes the world and a human life worth the trouble is not reserved for specialists, scholars or people who have been given this special task by the church. 'Worldly people', too, those who live and survive in the midst of the world, can and must also do this in their own way, in the place where their existence is now played out. Master Dirc assumes that they too, and in their own strength, must order their lives so that these become godly, and he wants to give them support in doing this. In the preface, addressed to Count Albert van Beieren, in whose service he was, Master Dirc writes that he has written his book 'in your honour', so that Albert will 'come to learn to know and to practise God his creator and abstain from sin'. Albert died soon after Dirc's *Tafel van den Kersten Ghelove* was finished, but the text found its way to many pious men and women who wanted to bring order to their lives and needed theological training and support to do so. These were people who, as Master Dirc presupposes of Count Albert, wanted to get to know their God and creator and honour him with what they did.

Dirc van Delf was a religious specialist – a priest and a monk and a scholar. He studied at different faculties abroad and gained a doctorate in theology. It seems logical to think that he regarded the writing of his book primarily as the fulfilment of his vocation and the exercise of his office and profession: namely to give instruction. But at the bottom of one of the first pages of the copy that he offered to Count Albert, there is a small drawing of him. The little man in the Dominican habit is almost a figure from a strip cartoon, since from his mouth comes a scroll containing the text 'Give me, Lord, true faith'. Master Dirc van Delf, whose priestly task is to preach, who as a member of a recognized monastic order is thought to be an expert in the sphere of religion, and for whom as a doctor of theology the Christian tradition needs to be familiar ground, evidently realizes that in the end of the day his situation is no different from that of his readers. He does not suppose that he has something that they need to have and that he can therefore give them. In his eyes, they and he are ultimately striving by different means for the same end: for true faith and a good life, for a righteous existence directed towards what is holy and wholesome.

In other words, for Master Dirc, being a Dominican, being a member of the Order of Preachers, evidently does not mean that he should form part of the guild of those who possess knowledge. To be a Dominican is to belong in one's own way to the community of those who seek and question, of those who are expectant and think critically.

Religious life for lay people

In his modest way Dirc van Delf gives form to what historians of religion regard as the main line in the activity of the first generations of Dominicans. They form part of a broad reform movement in the church which from the eleventh century contributed in word and deed, in writing and activity, towards liberating the holy on the one hand from the monasteries which had parted company with the world, and on the other from the closed circles of a church religion which was strictly regulated, formal and hierarchical. They perceived the traces of God again in the everyday world of ordinary men and women, as the biblical stories do. The religious life that they led did not consist in detaching themselves from everyday existence, but in honouring and having compassion on their neighbour, in humility and love, as trusting disciples of the poverty of Jesus Christ. This is regularly lost sight of in Dominican history. At the same time, down the centuries ordinary women and men have recognized themselves afresh in this message. They have found their own way and equipped themselves, some actually by reading Master Dirc van Delf's book.

Only a few witnesses to these people have survived. Most of them were not used to writing and in any case were not among those whose words had authority and therefore were handed on to later generations. However, anyone in search of them can find traces of them and what moved them in history. Thus in the first period of the Dominican movement the veneration of Mary Magdalene is striking: Mary was the woman who according to the New Testament sat at Jesus' feet during his lifetime, who anointed his feet before his death, who was the first to see him after his death, and who proclaimed his resurrection to the other disciples. In 1297 Mary Magdalene became the official *protectrix ordinis* of the Dominicans, patron saint of the Order. Out of veneration for her it proves that from the beginning Dominicans identified with the combination of listening to and following Jesus in which this woman led the way. In the late Middle Ages she was regarded as the embodiment of active compassion for suffering and the proclamation of God's boundless faithfulness. In particular the striking fact that the Dominican movement so emphatically sees itself reflected in a woman makes it clear that from a Dominican perspective, contact with the holy does not come about through a close connection with the leaders of the church and their view of the Christian tradition. The holy is encountered in everyday existence and the traces which appear in it of God, who according to the biblical writings is the Holy One.

Women in the Dominican movement

Because it is usually impossible for women to play a leading role in the hierarchical church forms of religion, throughout history they, in particular, have been very inventive in developing all kinds of forms of religious life in their own way and on their own conditions. They have ordered their everyday existence in ways appropriate to their often limited possibilities, which at the same time do justice to their longing for a dedicated and hallowed existence. It was not thought appropriate for women to speak in public, certainly not on religious matters – 'women are to remain quiet in the assemblies' writes the apostle Paul (I Corinthians 14.34), and 'during instruction, a woman should be quiet and respectful' (I Timothy 2.11) – but nevertheless some did succeed here. Speaking with kindred spirits or writing letters to them, quite often they succeeded in gathering a larger or smaller group around them. And although it was not thought appropriate for women themselves to call social or church institutions into existence, some succeeded in gaining official recognition for their groups.

But when this happened – many did not succeed or even strive for such recognition – the role which women themselves played here often remained concealed. This is as much the case in Dominican history as it is in that of the other great religious movements. Thus the official Dominican history relates that women played an important role at the beginning of the Dominican movement and that the first monastery that Dominic founded in 1206 was a women's convent, Prouille, in the south of France. According to the official history, however, he did this in order to receive women who turned to his preaching in reaction to the Catharism to which they had previously adhered (I shall be returning in the next chapter to Catharism and the significance that it has in Dominican history). However, once the Dominican Order was founded, the women's convent in Prouille proved to be far more than a reception area for women who had nowhere else to go. Just as they were first partners in the Cathar mission, so now they became partners in the Dominican mission.

This is also true of the women in the Dominican women's communities in San Sisto, Madrid and Bologna which were founded a short time later. Their houses played an important role as ports of call and bases for the itinerant brothers, in both the physical and the spiritual sense. We are told above all how the men instructed the women, but on close inspection it proves that the women encouraged and supported the men just as much. It is also striking that women fought hard to gain official recognition within the Dominican movement. That recognition finally came is to an important degree due to the efforts of Diana of Andalo, who had a friendship with Dominic, and above all with his successor Jordan of Saxony. However, she did not obtain by any means as dominant a place in written Dominican history as did, for example, Clare in Franciscan history. (The formal recognition that women could be part of the Dominican Order meant that they had to observe the church prohibition against preaching) That was ironic and painful for a movement which wanted to be an Order of proclamation and preaching. Moreover everything indicates that by contrast a women like Diana envisaged communities of women who also followed Mary Magdalene in presenting in public their own knowledge as believers of salvation and the holy.

Like their colleagues in other church movements, in the first period of the formal existence of their Order the Dominican authorities constantly fought against what they call 'whores and frivolous girls' who 'cut off their hair and put on the habit without supervision'. On the one hand this makes it clear that in Dominican circles, too, the prevalent opinion was that women were dangerous in principle, had to be put under the supervision of male authorities and, as Paul says, must not preach. On the other hand, the dispute about women also shows that they did indeed preach, evidently stimulated by the manner in which Dominican spirituality combines preaching with the way in which people in the midst of everyday life encounter the wholesome and holy. So these women in particular are the forebears of the men and women who are now trying to encounter the holy and speak of it in their own lives.

✝ The story of Thecla

Thinking of the future of the religious life in general and the Dominican tradition in particular, in my view it is extremely important to see the substantial place which women occupy in its history. The story of Thecla seems eminently suitable for opening our eyes to this.

This story, which dates from the second half of the second century, tells of a young woman from Iconium who came under the spell of the apostle Paul. His message about Jesus of Nazareth as God's anointed made it clear to her that she could have another life than life in submission to the demands that society otherwise made on women, as the spouse of her fiancé Thamyris. The fact that she opted for this other life and did not want to marry led to her being persecuted by her mother, her fiancé and ultimately by the authorities. However, time and again she escaped them in a miraculous way.

Paul mainly distanced himself from Thecla. He did not take her seriously in her quest for a better life and did not believe in her ability to remain steadfast in the midst of difficulties, though she constantly showed that she could. Despite her repeated requests he did not want to baptize her. When she finally stood in the arena before the wild animals which were about to devour her, she had no alternative but to baptize herself in a great basin of water that she happened to find there. 'In the name of Jesus Christ I baptize myself.' Paul might not have listened, but Thecla, the person who wrote down her story and, according to this story, also those who saw her activities, knew that she stood in the tradition of the liberating God which breaks through all limits, the God whom Paul preached. With this insight Thecla solemnly associates herself with this tradition and after she has escaped the threats of the arena, again in a miraculous way, proclaims to Paul that the God who gave him the power to preach had given her the power to baptize herself. Only now does Paul listen to her story, and he and Thecla agree that it is her task, too, to teach the word of God. But she had been doing that all the time, and with success.

It does not seem to be an exaggeration to say that the story of Thecla is the hidden story of the religious life. It is the story of those who according to the existing system of values are outsiders, but from this position gain new insights, who see new aspects of God and new signs of divine providence and devote themselves to these signs. The history of the religious life is the history of the ever new forms of dedication which come into being here, the story of the ways of ordering life which take form in the midst of everyday existence. The story of Thecla shows that the history of the religious life is to a large degree the history of the resolve of men and women to take their own experiences and intuitions seriously, even if others do not do so − indeed even if those who are supposed to be in authority do not do so.

The church father Tertullian praised the author of the story of Thecla because he was trying to honour Paul. But in his view he − or she, though evidently Tertullian could not conceive that the author could be a woman − had gone too far in suggesting that women should be able to baptize and preach. Anyone who is in search of religious life for laity will tend in a similar way to 'go too far' by existing criteria, even by criteria which are generally valid within the Dominican movement.

Nevertheless, it also seems to be in line with Dominican tradition to go beyond the boundaries in this way. The Dominican movement not only includes people who according to Catholic canon law are officially 'religious' and live in priories, but almost from the beginning included people who were 'lay': not priests, not religious, not leading a monastic existence, but living in the midst of the world and without any special church dignity. In 1285 this became official, but even earlier there were groups of men and women who tried to give form to a dedicated life in the Dominican spirit at the place where they happened to live and in their own specific circumstances. The French Dominican Henri-Dominique Lacordaire, who, as we saw earlier, refounded the Dominicans as a religious order halfway through the nineteenth century, thought that this lay movement was needed to make the Order truly complete. By founding a brotherhood of preachers – Lacordaire as yet had little of an eye for the history of the sisters – Dominic, in Lacordaire's eyes, freed the religious from their isolation and separation, and entrusted them with the important task of preaching in the world. But the fact that laity too have a place in the Dominican movement

> brought the religious life into the bosom of the family and to the nuptial bed ... It was no longer believed that it was necessary to flee the world in order to imitate the saints; every room could become a cell and every house a hermitage.

According to Lacordaire, the deeper the penetration into daily life in the midst of the world, the more one can speak of a truly Dominican life.

If he is right here – and in the next chapters I hope that it will become even more clear how right he is – then the Dominican tradition requires to be taken up and interpreted by 'lay people'. In other words, it needs to take a new form in an existence which is part of the everyday effort to live and survive in a worthwhile way and in the process to be dedicated to the holy. This is an existence which is an organic part of a world extending from the global society to one's own back garden; from the economy and politics to personal relations; from paid and voluntary work in society and church to love life and sex life in whatever form. If Lacordaire is right, then the Dominican tradition urgently needs new 'Theclas' who, in their own way, in their own situation, begin to lead a religious life in the footsteps of the Dominicans; who discover what these footsteps can be in everyday circumstances and try out where they lead them. It needs people who take their discoveries seriously enough also to talk about them and let others share in them.

2

With the Eyes of a Living Soul: Dominican spirituality

In 1967 the sculptress Anne Hofte made a sculpture which since then has stood above the entrance to the town hall of Haarlem. It commemorates the Dominican presence in this city. It portrays Dominic not as an isolated man, standing by himself. As she sees him, he forms almost a single whole with those who are on their way after him and with him, so much so that what she has made seems almost to be one body with three clearly different heads.

Anne Hofte has had a key insight here. It is indeed impossible to detach the figure of Dominic from the people around him. What he strove for as a person to a large degree corresponded with the development of the Dominican movement, the formation of a community which was completely orientated on preaching. When his successor as Master General, Jordan of Saxony, wrote a book thirteen years after Dominic's death about the origin of the Order of Preachers, which had by then been recognized by the church, no more than half his text was devoted to Dominic. Moreover it is remarkable how far, in the picture which Jordan paints of him, Dominic is from occupying a central position in early Dominican history. He always operates on a second level and reacts above all to the initiative of others.† One of his striking characteristics seems to be this particular reluctance to focus attention on his person and to formulate a fixed programme which then needs only to be carried out. The very way in which he wants to avoid being the determining factor is typical of his leadership.

But it is certainly also the case that without Dominic there would have been no Dominican movement. Some basic features of what can be called 'Dominican spirituality' can be found in him. These include an eye for the situation and a pragmatic matter-of-factness, combined with a strong desire to order life in such a way that in the given circumstances it is wholesome and points to the God of salvation.

Dominic

According to the tradition, Dominic was born Domingo de Guzmán around 1170 in Spanish Castile, around 100 miles north of Madrid. The son of a minor landowner, he was able to study, which at this time almost automatically meant that he would become a cleric. After his ordination to the priesthood he became a canon at the cathedral of Osma; in other words, he lived his life largely within a community whose task it was to perform the liturgy in the diocesan church, with due dignity and according to the rules. One story to which I shall be returning relates how when Dominic was on a journey with his bishop Diego in 1203, in Toulouse he met an innkeeper who, like many others in this region, held views which were being proclaimed by the so-called Cathars. These deviated from Catholic Christianity. Dominic spent the whole night with him discussing these views, which were regarded as heretical. The story has it that the next evening the innkeeper was convinced of the Catholic truth. Moreover Dominic had inwardly said farewell to his life as a canon which, orientated on the liturgy, prayer and the wealth of the church tradition, was remote from the daily struggle to exist waged by ordinary people. The desire had been aroused in him to preach against prevailing abuses and the misunderstandings which threatened. He wanted to make it clear both to the established church and to those who turned their backs on the church because of the abuses which they felt to be prevalent there what the wholesome meaning of a genuine Christian faith could be.

In a number of intermediary stages he was first sent out by Pope Innocent III, with Bishop Diego and some others, to restore the Cathars in the south of France to the Catholic faith through preaching. Above all, thanks to Diego, the group did not display the outward pomp that ecclesiastical dignitaries usually showed. That only provoked the antipathy and the fury of the Cathars, who saw themselves as a true, poor church, following Jesus and the apostles. After Diego's sudden death Dominic began a new group of preachers in Toulouse with the support of Fulco, the local bishop. In 1216 this community was recognized as an independent religious fellowship by Pope Honorius III.

But this was not enough for Dominic. According to the chronicle of early Dominican history by Jordan of Saxony, he envisaged a movement as 'an order which in name and nature would be an order of preachers'. He strove for papal approval with great stubbornness, and some weeks after the first recognition of his small company, at the beginning of 1217, this community did indeed receive from the pope a universal mission to preach:

> Because God, who always enriches his church with new growth, wanted to bring these modern times into accord with former times and with the Catholic faith, he has filled you with a holy desire to choose poverty, to live in a monastery, to be free for preaching the word of God and to proclaim the name of our Lord Jesus Christ throughout the world.

It is and remains striking that here we have a pope who shows himself grateful for the initiative of a small group of people and thinks that their emergence is of historic significance. Honorius evidently shared their view that there was an urgent need for good preaching combined with a credible presence. But it would only emerge gradually just how revolutionary the papal decision was to make preaching the task of a religious order for the first time in church history. For how did the freedom of these preachers relate to the authority of others in the church, especially that of the bishops, to whom above all, according to the tradition, the responsibility for preaching had been entrusted? Who was to determine what was correct preaching, appropriate to the situation? What was a credible approach, and how did the Dominican approach relate to that of other representatives of the church?

Dominic does not seem to have been much interested in this kind of question, important though it might have been from the perspective of church organization. His concern was to preach freedom in such a way that it again became clear that the Christian faith had a good, wholesome message to proclaim. Immediately after the papal recognition of his small group as the 'Order of Preachers', he sent out those who had gathered around him, two by two. Forced by the church authorities to adopt an existing monastic rule as the basis for their community, these companions chose the Rule of Augustine, because little was laid down in it and thus much could be supplied. In fact the members of the new 'Order of Preachers' treated Augustine's rule very freely. For example, Dominic does not seem to have been very bothered about the question whether his men, sent out in pairs, could continue to form a community that was 'one in heart and soul', which in Augustine's eyes was the central aim of the religious life. From a Dominican perspective, preaching itself is evidently so much the centre of ordering life that all other arrangements depend on it or are orientated on it, or at least they should be. It is typical in this connection that from the beginning, in the specifically Dominican regulations which have been added to the Rule of Augustine, there is the explicit stipulation that any regulation can be dispensed with if it hinders preaching. For, the reasoning goes, 'as is well known, our Order was originally founded specifically in order to preach'.

The world as a holy place

The orientation on preaching means that the Dominican identity does not lie in the past. Neither the will of Dominic nor the original form of the Dominican movement determines what is Dominican. The possibilities for preaching, the occasions there are for acting and speaking as an open book which points to God, in a current situation which constantly changes, are the determining factors for the Order. Dominic and his companions did not know where to begin in seeking to regard the religious life as a life wholly orientated on preaching in this sense and on what they called 'the salvation of souls': salvation, happiness, the spiritual well-being of men and women in the sight of God. How was a life to be ordered around these tasks? And even those who have only a superficial knowledge of Dominican history are given numerous indications that from the beginning there was intensive discussion about the focus and the best way of organizing a religious life which was wholly devoted to seeking traces of the God of salvation and bringing them to light. Given this aim, what was the significance of the religious life as the Catholic Church officially saw it: a life of poverty, celibacy and obedience? What was the meaning of leadership, and what significance could 'community' have for people who for a large part of their time were out on the road in pairs? What was religious life anyway if it did not assume the familiar form of separation from the world, but sought to stand in its very midst? The discussion of these and similar questions has never really stopped in Dominican circles. For the last 30 years it has been carried on with new intensity, by sisters and brothers and by lay people involved in the Dominican movement.

Here the Dominican orientation on preaching provides a specific perspective. For preaching calls for presence, not only for the obvious reasons that one must be with people to be able to talk to them and to do something for their welfare, but first of all because one must be amongst them to know what needs to be said and done. In the previous chapter we saw that being a true Dominican does not mean belonging to the guild of scholars. Being a true Dominican consists first and foremost in becoming part of the company of seekers and questioners, so as in this way, with the help of human reason and building on the Christian tradition, to find something of an answer. This means in principle breaking with any monastic self-sufficiency. Humbert of Romans, who was the Master General of the Dominicans from 1254 to 1263, made the point with all necessary clarity:

> Jesus Christ himself had no house where he could lay his head when he began to preach, but went through the villages and towns and through all of Galilee preaching. Nor did the apostles have houses of their own to live in: they went out into the world preaching everywhere. So what must we think of preachers who always want to stay at home in their monasteries?

As if God were to be found especially there, says Humbert. For everything turns on the question where traces of God are to be found. Where does the holy appear as a pointer to God's holiness? And how does one organize one's life around these places, looking for them and being alert to them? The quotation from Humbert of Romans suggests that it is of the essence of Dominican life time and again to go away from the tranquillity of one's house and to enter the unrest of the street and the inn, politics and journalism, welfare, teaching and science, in the belief that the holy, the traces of the Holy One, are to be found there.

It is not necessary to retreat from the world to encounter God – the source of all that exists, the support of our own existence and the goal desired by all that exists, towards which it is on its way. Being involved in the history of which we are a part, in what happens to those who are close to us, in what happens to us, is no hindrance to a true bond with God. So there is no need to break with these things either permanently, by going to live apart from the world, or temporarily, by shutting oneself off from the world with the help of particular techniques. Dominicans are convinced that the world in which we live, turbulent and restless, often violent and terrifying, is at the same time the place where the holy comes to light, the place where we encounter and listen to – 'contemplate' – God. We may ask what life is all about in the coffee bar or the theatre; we may find the answer to an all-important question or the insight which we have been seeking for so long while telephoning or reading a bedtime story to a child. Of course these questions and insights must be reflected on patiently, deepened in tranquillity and worked out with concentrated attention. But the material for reflection, which has to be deepened and worked out, is always offered by everyday life. It is therefore necessary to be open to everything.

A place where the holy is gathered together

In 1989, the supreme body of the Dominican brothers, the General Chapter, which assembled that year in Oakland in America, stated with the utmost clarity that according to the Dominican conviction the holy is primarily to be found in the world:

> We do not first contemplate and after that go out to others. To be called to preach is above all to be called to contemplate together with others, to listen, to take a place alongside those who understand God's word.

So the house and the community of like-minded colleagues is not the place where the Dominican religious life is especially led. On the contrary, a Dominican house is a place where the religious life that is lived out and found in so many places and moments is brought together. It is a place where this life is thought through, celebrated and meditated on, and in this way again is given a new impulse; it is a place where this life is explicitly laid before God, as the Mystery which cherishes and preserves all that is holy in the midst of everyday life.

I believe that a Dominican religious life in the specific sense takes form whenever such a house, such a space and such a place is created and kept in being. It can be represented by a group which lives together or a training centre, a church congregation or even a group of people who regularly meet together in a small hall or a living room. To live the religious life in the Dominican sense is to order one's own life, with all its facets, around such a place for meeting and celebrating, for reflecting and being sent out again.⟩In an extreme instance such a place can even be simply in one's own head and heart – what the Dominican mystic Catherine of Siena calls the 'cell of self-knowledge' – or on the pages within the covers of a notebook, or in a corner of one's own house. But usually it will involve a group of people who join together as far as they can to consider and seek, find calm and achieve clarity, become active and speak. In this sense countless people have led a religious life, and many people are leading a religious life at this very moment.

History shows that laity in particular – necessarily, since in their position they can hardly do otherwise – strongly maintain that a place of reflection and contemplation can be found and created in the midst of everyday existence. Some of them join larger or smaller communities which explicitly call themselves Dominican. In the statutes of one such community, dating from 1244, such laity are addressed as follows:

> Inspired by the example of St Dominic and confident of his help and support, you have joined together to devote yourselves to works of kindness, by which the wretchedness of the poor will be relieved and a service provided for the salvation of souls. We see how wonderful the Lord is in his saints. The example of only one man has been like a tiny seed sown in the ground, from which the Lord has raised up an abundant harvest of faithful souls.

And the same story is told in broad outline in the Rule which since 1987 has been officially regarded as the basis for communities of Dominican laity. The idea is that among the 'ordinary believers' in the church, all of whom are called 'to radiate the presence of Christ among the peoples so that the divine message of redemption is known and accepted everywhere', there are some 'who are moved by the holy Spirit to live according to the spirit and the charisma of St Dominic ...'

It is important to point out that this last sentence is unfinished. It goes on to say that these lay believers play a full part in the Order of Preachers. Thus according to the Dominican regulations Dominican laity are just as much Dominicans as fathers and sisters and nuns are, so it is clearly the Dominican conviction that it is not the conventual life that makes a life into a religious life. But the picture of our Dominican existence that is given here is one-sided. It overlooks too much the numerous Theclas from the Dominican past, whereas in the last chapter we established that it is the traces of the Theclas in particular which can be important for people today.

Lay people discover God's nearness

Lay people do not only become involved in the Dominican movement when they follow in the footsteps of Dominic and orientate their lives on God and therefore devote themselves to good works. Lay people stand at the origin of the idea that God can be encountered in everyday life, an idea which Dominic takes up in a specific way in founding his Order of Preachers and from which he draws specific conclusions.

In the twelfth and thirteenth centuries the power of secular and church leaders grew, but so too did the power of those who contributed to the economy of the cities. On the one hand this was a period of enrichment in every sense of the word, but as always that also meant impoverishment for all kinds of groups. Techniques improved and trade grew. The world seemed less threatening and became more and more a place where people could achieve a truly good life. This situation led to a profound re-reading of the Christian tradition, and especially the New Testament. Whereas some regarded the exercise of power and the occupation of a high position as a sign of godly dignity, and God's presence was above all experienced in the dignitaries of society or the church, a strikingly large number of others read with renewed attention the texts of the Gospels in which the poor and the little ones are those who are said to be blessed:

> You know that among the Gentiles the rulers lord it over them, and great men make their authority felt. Among you this is not to happen. No; anyone who wants to become great among you must be your servant, and anyone who wants to be first among you must be your slave (Matthew 20.25-28).

Whereas in the preceding period Jesus had often been presented as the unmoved, all-dominant Son of God, now he was rediscovered as the Son of man who had not come to be served but to serve. It was on the periphery of social power and at the periphery of the church, among women and other lay people, that people learned to regard life in dependence and serving in vulnerability as a godly dignity.

In this connection there was talk of *poenitentia*. Literally this Latin word means 'repentance', but at this time it pointed to the rediscovery of what in the New Testament is called *metanoia*, and which is usually translated as 'conversion'. So it denoted turning away from the prevailing but deeply false order of things and ordering one's life anew on the basis of the values which are expressed in the words and actions of Jesus: the blind see and the lame walk, lepers are cleansed and the deaf hear, the dead arise and good news is preached to the poor (Matthew 11.5). Christianity connects this with God, who already in the book of Exodus is said to see people's misery, hear their cries about their oppression and know their suffering (Exodus 3.7). Like the emergence of Petrus Waldes and Francis of Assisi, the emergence of Dominic was part of the broad quest for an authentic faith which embraced poverty and service, and in this way was liberating. In the time when Dominic founded his Order of Preachers, everywhere there were groups which lived a life of sisters and brothers of penitence – *poenitentia* – that made them turn their backs on existing conditions and seek a new life more in keeping with the God who comes to light in the words and actions of Jesus. When the Dominicans became an established religious order, some of these groups turned to the Dominicans for support. In 1285 that led the then Master General of the Dominican Order, Munio of Zamora, to give 'the brothers and sisters of penitence of St Dominic' a special lay task in the Dominican Order. However, this changed the character of these lay communities. As an official Dominican branch, the 'brothers and sisters of penitence' were – on paper, at any rate – markedly dependent on the Dominicans who were priests and religious under Catholic canon law.

'Like the apostles'

So over broad areas during the twelfth and thirteenth centuries people sought to live a life in accordance with the gospel (*vita evangelica*), a life that was at one with the gospel that they had learned to read from the perspective of the poor Jesus. It was also called a *vita apostolica*, a life like that of the apostles.

Two ideas play a role in this last expression, both of which are important for a Dominican spirituality. First there is the description of the life of the apostles shortly after Jesus' death and resurrection in the fourth chapter of the Acts of the Apostles. This was already often the basis of a movement for the renewal of the religious life, and Augustine's Rule also refers emphatically to it:

> The whole group of believers was united, heart and soul; no one claimed private ownership of any possessions, as everything they owned was held in common (Acts 4.32).

On the basis of this idea of *vita apostolica,* new communities came into being, but above all existing religious houses and even whole religious orders were re-formed. The second idea of *vita apostolica* comes from the story of Jesus sending out his apostles, as this is described in the tenth chapter of the Gospel according to Matthew. In it we are told that Jesus sent out his disciples with the following commission:

> And as you go, proclaim that the kingdom of Heaven is close at hand. Cure the sick, raise the dead, cleanse those suffering from virulent skin diseases, drive out devils. You received without charge, give without charge. Provide yourselves with no gold or silver, not even with coppers for your purses, with no haversack for the journey or spare tunic or footwear or a staff, for the labourer deserves his keep (Matthew 10.7-10).

This was read as: speak about the kingdom of God and let what this means be seen by what you do and how you live; put what you are talking about into practice in a way which fits the local situation; do not base yourself on formal authority or church power, nor be clothed in riches; show in all nakedness what you stand for and in this way associate yourself with people to whom the good news according to the Gospel is first preached; be convinced that you can truly live in this way. A colourful set of movements large and small began on the basis of this second notion of *vita apostolica;* a number of them eventually ran into difficulties because in the eyes of the secular or church authority they exceeded their brief. This might happen, for example, because lay members were preaching the faith, whereas preaching was officially reserved for priests; so in the official view, what lay people, and above all what women said, simply could not be in accord with the true faith.

The itinerant preaching of Diego and Dominic in the south of France, and later that of members of the little group that formed around Dominic in Toulouse, was primarily a form of *vita apostolica* in this second sense. The special feature was that Dominic, like

Francis, ultimately succeeded in making it clear to the church authorities that this way of preaching, which was usually associated with dissident – heretical – groups, was really the most authentic form of Christian preaching. For not only was he able to attract enough people in a short time to create a powerful religious community with settlements in many places, but he also convinced the pope of the need of the kind of itinerant preaching that he and his people stood for.

Equality in the midst of difference

Dominic succeeded in combining the two notions of *vita apostolica*. In this way his community of preachers succeeded in gaining recognition as an authentic form of religious life. In so doing he took into account the fact that there was no break here with the idea that 'religious' constitute a special state in the church, different from others, and with a specific form of life which has its own laws and rules. Nevertheless, the simple fact that so many groups were striving for a *vita apostolica* in the second sense represented powerful opposition to the idea that religious should in principle be different from other people.

Moreover, Dominic had in view an order of trained preachers who were familiar with developments in theology and biblical exegesis. In the conditions of the Middle Ages this automatically meant that his Order had to consist of priests. By taking this option Dominic prevented conflicts breaking out even more quickly than they already had over the right of Dominicans to preach wherever their mission brought them, and doubts about their orthodoxy arising all too soon. The history of earlier movements probably led Dominic to conclude that a preaching Order in which the actual preaching was not reserved to priests would never gain official recognition. It seems not to have been a real problem to him that the consequence of his choice was that only unmarried men could be full members of this Order. But it was a consequence of this that the membership of women as contemplatives, and much later as active sisters, and the membership of laity involved in the Order, ultimately remained a derivative membership.

But there was always also a counter-movement. The person who in 1262 wrote in the statutes of a local Dominican lay community that 'there is no difference in the eyes of God between men and women' and therefore that they needed to have the same rights and duties in the communities was following a Dominican logic. At the same time he went much further than Dominic and his successors, or the Dominican regulations, usually go or can go, given the conditions in the church. However, it is striking that those who laid down these statutes gave no indication of any sense that they were introducing something revolutionary. That leads me to suppose that already in the thirteenth century more equality was achieved than the official regulations indicate. If this is true, then all those Dominicans who in our time strive for equality in the midst of all differences – social equality, church equality and equality within their own Order – stand in a tradition which is as old as the Dominican movement itself.

The conversation with the innkeeper

Francesco Bernadone was to a large degree a kindred spirit of Domingo de Guzmán. Like him he presided over the birth of a new religious family within the broad twelfth- and thirteenth-century quest for a true 'life according to the gospel' and a 'life according to the apostles'. He states very clearly and explicitly the experience that in his view stands at the start of it all. In 1226, at the end of his life, the man who would come to be known as Saint Francis of Assisi wrote in his 'Testament':

> This is how God inspired me, Brother Francis, to embark upon a life of penance. When I was in sin, the sight of lepers nauseated me beyond measure; but then God himself led me into their company, and I had pity on them. When I had once become acquainted with them, what had previously nauseated me became a source of spiritual and physical consolation for me.

The sight of a leper, really *seeing* someone who had nothing but his sickness and his abhorrence, changed Francis' whole life. From then on, he felt that what was holy and divine in this life could no longer exist in wealth and glittering abundance, but only in weak humanity. God comes in a suffering figure, emptied of almost all quasi-divine dignity: Francis also saw this in the Gospel stories about the poor and suffering Jesus and his apostles, in whose footsteps he walked with his companions, poor and unprotected.

It is significant that no such testament of Dominic has been handed down to us. So Dominicans must themselves find and tell the story that in their eyes expresses the core of his life and Dominican spirituality. The story of Dominic's nocturnal discussion with the innkeeper with whom he was lodging in Toulouse, which I have already referred to, can become the parable of a central Dominican intuition. The first thing that is striking about this story – and it is by no means unimportant – is that it is set in the street and in the pub. The events take place in the midst of the feverish energy which is part of the world of living and surviving, the all-embracing and all-permeating struggle for power and reputation, even in the thirteenth century. Dominic is not in the inn as one who is engaged on an exalted religious mission, but as the companion of his bishop Diego, who had been given the task of negotiating in the name of his king in Denmark over a possible bride for the king's son. This was the kind of political task which could befall a bishop at this time and which needed to be negotiated tactfully. It was on the periphery of the ordinary course of events that the decisive encounter took place. That too seems characteristic.

Nothing has come down to us about the content of Dominic's nocturnal discussion with the innkeeper. But they will most probably have talked about the fact that the innkeeper no longer wanted to belong to the Catholic Church and had gone over to the true church of the Cathars. At this time Catharism was a developed religious system with a teaching and organization of its own, which in the south of France had a substantial following both among the people and among the local leaders. Its power of attraction lay above all in the fact that the Cathars, in contrast to the Catholic Church with its power and riches, presented themselves as the true church, as the real followers of the poor Jesus of the gospel. They were convinced that they were the only ones who were really walking in the footsteps of the apostles. The innkeeper doubtless indicated to Dominic his abhorrence of the wealth and power of the church, an abhorrence that was shared by many. He bore witness to the feeling that the church is unfaithful to itself when those who hold office in it behave like 'the rulers of the peoples', although Jesus said that he did not want things to be like this among his followers. It is conceivable that this convinced Dominic that credible preaching can take place only in poverty and vulnerability.

Certainly the innkeeper also said something about the Cathar doctrine. Opposing the Catholic Church, which in their eyes had become too worldly, the Cathars preached that people could be happy and feel themselves close to God only if they succeeded in distancing themselves from all that was bodily, material and earthly. They needed to detach themselves from their fatal bond to all these things, to free themselves from desires for food, clothing and sexuality. In the Cathar view all that was material stood infinitely far from God, and it was the task of human beings to live exclusively for the soul and also to be free of all things. In the Cathar movement, those who succeeded in doing this were regarded as 'perfect', and were seen as leaders and pioneers.

Once again, the tradition says nothing about this. But I imagine that Dominic drew the innkeeper's attention to the paradox in the teaching of the church to which he belonged. On the one hand the Cathars evidently complained about the behaviour of the Catholic Church and its representatives, and about the injustice that was the result of this. On the other hand, they based this criticism on a doctrine which proclaimed that everything that happens to human beings in a bodily sense is ultimately unimportant and has no real significance; that they must learn to dissociate themselves from it. As I imagine the conversation, Dominic will have tried to make the innkeeper see that in the life of Jesus as the Gospels relate it there is no question of distancing oneself from the material. I imagine how during his exposition he himself also began to see more and more clearly that in the biblical view God's holiness does not lie in the distance between divine exaltation and human insignificance. According to the biblical notion, God's holiness lies precisely in God's involvement in human fortunes. God is bound up with our bodily history, our pain, our desire; and the face of this God is shown in the life of Jesus:

> He went round ... teaching in their synagogues, proclaiming the good news of the kingdom and curing all kinds of disease and illness among the people (Matthew 4.23; cf. 9.35).

The God to whom Jesus gives expression is not close to detached souls, but to human life in all its bodily nature, in which the good breaks through with all its vulnerability.

According to the tradition, in his nocturnal conversation with the innkeeper Dominic convinced him that the Cathar doctrine was false teaching. But I can also imagine that while he was debating, Dominic also discovered how important the biblical message of

God's nearness really was. Even as he spoke, he began to realize the degree to which according to the biblical tradition God is present, near and involved. In my view Dominic therefore did not leave his secluded, harmonious life in the capital, Osma, only out of a sense of duty, because his conversation with the innkeeper made him see how necessary preaching against the Cathars was. Dominic began to preach because while he was talking to the innkeeper he discovered that God is not primarily present in a harmony cut off from the world, but precisely where things matter to people in the world, where it is decided whether their fate will be good or bad. God is bound up with that fate.

At the end of the fourteenth century the Dominican and painter Fra Angelico on one occasion depicted Dominic standing before a crucified Christ with his hand over his eyes. It is as if Dominic cannot not believe that the divine could be so earthly, the most exalted be so lowly and submissive, the most powerful be so prepared to be hurt and injured.

With the eyes of a living soul

If Dominican spirituality has a core, then it would be this insight into the unexpected and unheard-of nearness of God, despite and in the midst of all our experiences of distance from God, of circumstances that cry out to God, of godforsakenness. It is this nearness which makes religion possible, and with it religious life, not religion in the sense of holding fast to a tradition, a legalistic morality or lofty ceremonies, but religion as the Nigerian-British author Ben Okri has written about it: as the capacity to hear the voice of creation, to be spoken to by the storm, to be breathed on by the thunder, to be driven by human suffering, moved by flowers, spoken to by words. In our world, shockingly little attention is paid to human suffering; animals, plants and things are treated as if they had no intrinsic value; and the capacity to see what is really happening is not only an undeveloped but even an underestimated virtue. In this situation the message that the traces of God's holiness lie in what comes to light as holy in everyday life means that true spirituality consists especially in openness, attentiveness and the capacity to be touched.

Humbert of Romans writes that in order to be able to preach well in the Dominican sense of the word, in both word and deed it is necessary above all to be a good contemplative. Here Humbert does not use the term 'contemplative' in the usual sense, as a designation for someone who in silence and segregation steeps himself in the divine and tries to find it deep within himself. For Humbert contemplation is in fact openness, attentiveness and the capacity to be touched. What is necessary on the spiritual journey that one takes is insight into one's own situation, into the state of the world around one and one's own place in it. Therefore, according to Humbert, to live by a Dominican spirituality means to live with eyes on all sides. He says that it is like the four mysterious 'living, ensouled beings' who are mentioned in the first chapter of the book of Ezekiel:

> Now, as I looked at the living creatures, I saw a wheel touching the ground beside each of the four-faced living creatures . . . When the living creatures moved, in which ever of the four directions they moved, they did not need to turn as they moved. Their circumference was of awe-inspiring size, and the rims of all four had eyes. When the living creatures moved, the wheels moved beside them (Ezekiel 1.15-19).

In Ezekiel these four living, animate beings with their wheels which have eyes are the symbol of God's nearness to all that is, of God's involvement in what happens, of God's all-permeating and all-embracing concern.

Dominican life is life in their footsteps, living with the eyes of a living soul, and becoming a trace of God along this way. Those who live by a Dominican spirituality commit themselves to being a living soul in the midst of living souls. Their lives are a matter of seeing, being moved by what happens, and in turn being inspired by this movement. It is a way of ordering existence in such a way that it points only to a divine involvement. This can take infinite forms, depending on time and place, personal circumstances and one's own character. But those who order their lives in this way ultimately form a community which in the Dominican sense is 'one heart and one soul', in the words of the Rule of Augustine.

3

Teresa's Fury, Catherine's Passion: Contemplation in action

To contemplate in the Dominican sense is to look with the eyes of a living soul. It is to allow ourselves to be touched by what happens to us and the world around, in the belief that in this way we come upon traces of the God of salvation and liberation.

However, that is a paradoxical belief. Those who allow themselves to be touched often do not immediately become happier and do not always have the feeling that everything is borne up by a wholesome and holy presence. The Algerian writer Assia Djebar allowed herself to be touched above all by the fate of women in her land, in former times and now, and wrote a book with the evocative title *So Vast the Prison*. When she tries to sum up what she is left with after her journey through all the stories of women who have been taken away and tortured, who have died and been murdered, she says:

> I do not cry, I am the cry. The whole way leads past the rubbish heaps of yesterday's war, past the inexpressible terrors of today ... I do not cry, I am the cry, carried along in an urgent and blind flight. The white procession of spectres behind me becomes an army that pursues me: then the words of the disappeared become a language which comes to life again, while the men already wave their arms over the field where the dead, or their masked shadows, live.

Nothing remains but a cry, but Djebar is convinced that this cry is not meaningless. She quotes a poem by the French poet Jeanne Hyvrard, who says, as she balances on a knife edge:

You say that suffering has no use.
But it has.
It serves to make you cry.
To
make you attentive to the madness,
To
make you attentive to the way the world
is going to pieces.

Those who cry, those who become a cry, at the deepest level do not express despair but hope, and have become hope in the despair. Anyone who is touched and wounded by what happens and is convinced that it makes sense to be touched, lives in the presence of God. God's nearness does not lie directly in the pain but in the hope for something better, the love of life and the belief that another, more divine-human, existence must be possible.

So to contemplate in the Dominican sense is to see, but above all also to see in the dark:

They are there, the stars,
only it is not always dark enough
to see them,

writes the Dutch theologian and poet Vera Huijgen. That you must be in the dark to see the true light, that the grain of wheat must die in order to bring forth fruit, as Jesus says in the Gospel of John (12.24), remains a mystery. But that mystery forms the heart of the religious life in the Christian sense, and also in the Dominican sense.

Teresa's fury

To begin with, a story by the Jewish writer Alexandro Jodorowsky can help us get a better view of this mystery. At first sight this story above all makes it clear why in our time many people find a problem in putting themselves in the line of the biblical, Jewish and Christian traditions. But in the second instance the story proves to offer us surprising points of contact for living with this tradition in a new way, one which joins up with the previous chapter about Dominican spirituality.

Alexandro Jodorowsky was born in Chile and now lives in Paris. He comes from a family of Ukrainian and Lithuanian Jews. He writes about his ancestors and begins with a story which is called

'Teresa's Fury'. This story starts like this:

> In 1903 my grandmother Teresa got cross with God and all the Jews
> from Dneiperpropetrovsk in the Ukraine who continued to believe in
> Him despite the fatal flooding of the Dnieper. In the flood her favourite
> son José lost his life. When the water began to flood into the house the
> boy pulled a chest into the living room and climbed on to it, but the
> chest didn't float because it was full of the thirty-seven treatises of the
> Talmud.

The Talmud is, of course, the written account of the Jewish
tradition. Here a vivid picture is given of our relationship to the
religious tradition. Our history – first and foremost, of course,
Jewish history, but also the history of others; history within but also
outside Europe – and our violent time is full of Josés and therefore
full of grandmother Teresas. In countless situations – in world
history and on a domestic, common-or-garden scale – people have
been deceived in the support that they sought from the stories of the
Bible and their authoritative exposition. We all know examples of
people who were not helped much by climbing on the chests of the
tradition in their battle to survive in the 'formlessness and void' of
our history which crops up time and again. We all know examples
of people who because of their religious ties sank all the more
quickly into the chaos around them or in their soul.

But Jodorowsky does not stop here. He suggests that a new
contact with tradition becomes possible from the bottom of
nothingness. With clear satisfaction he relates how his grandmother
with her surviving children and her husband enters the synagogue,
and how there she interrupts the reading of Leviticus 19: 'Speak to
the whole assembly of the Israelites and say to them . . .'. She cries
out: 'I shall say something to you.' Jodorowsky relates how she
enters the part of the house of prayer which is forbidden to women,
pushes aside the men, presses her mouth to the scroll and screams at
the letters:

> Your books lie. They say that you saved all the people, that you divided
> the Red Sea with the same ease that I cut my carrots, yet you didn't do
> anything for my poor José . . . That innocent child had nothing on his
> conscience, so what did you want to show me? That your power is
> boundless? I know that. That you are an impenetrable mystery and that I
> must show my faith by calmly accepting this crime? Never. That is
> something for prophets of the stature of Abraham who can put a knife to

their children's throats, but not for a poor woman like me.

This is a woman who wears her heart on her sleeve and in her anger finds the courage to speak on the authority of her own experience.

But there is even more. In this story we do not just hear the umpteenth agonized protest against the excess of suffering in human history and the heart-rending lament that time and again this protest seems to be in vain. Jodorowsky's story about his grandmother Teresa makes clear how in this protest again a trace of God's holiness can be found.

Courage

There is a good reason why Teresa's outburst in Jodorowsky's story interrupts the reading of Leviticus 19 in particular. Leviticus 19 begins with the central divine command for Israel: 'Be holy, for I, the Mighty One your God, am holy.' Israel must observe the commandments which follow in this chapter and in the Hebrew Bible as a whole, or those which are later derived from them in the Jewish tradition, as a sign that it is God's people, that in its holiness it is the reflection of God's holiness.

Jodorowsky describes how his grandmother Teresa attacks the text of Leviticus 19 in her fury: she presses 'her sharp face against the parchment of the Torah ... and [cries out] at the Hebrew letters'. Here Jodorowsky is suggesting that her words mingle with the written letters and that in a sense her cry takes the place of the text. Her everyday sentences and her living anger mix with the words of the Holiness Code written on parchment. As Jodorowsky describes it, it is clear that for him Teresa's anger can be the content and indeed take the place of the Holiness Code in Leviticus 19: 'Be holy, for I, the Mighty One your God, am holy,' is the fundamental commandment of Leviticus 19. This commandment is in fact formulated anew in the story of Teresa's fury. It now runs: Be furious as Teresa is furious. Do not succumb to the wave of uncertainty and change, of violence and oppression. In the fight with the chaos that is life, do not trust blindly in the tradition, as Teresa's son José did. Trust in your anger and your fury; your urge to survive and the cunning that emerges from it.

'Teresa's Fury' is in the first instance a typically Jewish story. This is not only because it reacts to Jewish history, which more than any other has been played out in the shadow of our violent twentieth century, but also because it builds on a specific Jewish tradition. Within Judaism the complaint out of love for God's creation about what happens, the complaint about powers which cause suffering and destruction, even when the complainant turns against God himself; the complaint against God out of love for God's creation and God's glory and holiness in this creation, are regarded as a form of piety. But Teresa's fury leads her to give up her Jewishness. She leaves the closed community and with her family tries to survive in her own strength, as one human being among others. Thus 'Teresa's Fury' becomes a story for and about the human situation. Jodorowsky's tale is finally about his ancestors' art of survival, about the miraculous art of survival among Jews in general and of course among human beings in general, though they are constantly overwhelmed by poverty, violence, sickness and bad luck. I think that by depicting how Teresa screams at the letters of the Bible Jodorowsky is in fact presenting his story as a chronicle of the holy. He may not perhaps put the stories that he hears and tells on quite the same level as the Bible, but they are certainly on the same level as the commentaries in the Talmud. However, he thinks that his stories do not leave people in the lurch at crucial moments and do not drag them down. They give people courage to swim.

Those who read the stories that Jodorowsky tells, the stories which countless other writers tell, which are told in countless places, will learn to see with their own eyes that people in their stubborn attempts to survive in a decent way and to help others to survive in a decent way are holy as the Mighty One their God is holy. Or, to put it another way, Jodorowsky's grandmother Teresa can help us to contemplate in the Dominican sense of the word.

Passion out of divine compassion

In the view of the mediaeval Dominican theologian Thomas Aquinas (c. 1225-74), it is in the world in which we live that people can encounter God's holiness. The God of salvation in whom we hope in our longing to become whole, whom we love in our quest and in whom we thus believe, can be already seen and experienced in our life. In order to make that happen, Aquinas thinks that it is necessary to adopt a specific viewpoint towards the world. Hearing and reading stories which have been handed down and told from the past, above all the biblical stories, serves to develop the perspective – Thomas speaks of the 'light of faith' that must shine in believers – which we need in order to perceive the divine presence.

In my view the story of Jodorowsky's grandmother Teresa deserves to be handed down by people in search of a Dominican spirituality in the way in which I am describing it here. Those who walk in the footsteps of grandmother Teresa re-read what comes to us from the past with the human longing for a truly good life and the dogged human determination to achieve it. It opens up the biblical writings in a new way. Spurred on by our own pain and our fury at the pain of others, we read in the Old or First Testament about an involved Presence, in solidarity with us and therefore liberating; and in the New or Second Testament we read about the concentration of this presence in the words and actions, in the life, death and resurrection of Jesus of Nazareth, who has been called God's anointed. And strengthened by what we are told in this way, we go on to look and listen to the world which is ours. 'Be holy, as I the Mighty One your God am holy', as my voice resounds in the concern and respect that sometimes take form in the creation, as my face shines in the concern and the respect that people and things require but often do not get. This is a holiness which, where it comes to life, deserves to be celebrated and praised; where it remains hidden it requires to be stubbornly confessed. For despite everything, this is the power that sustains all that exists, and where it seems to be lacking it spurs people on to invoke it in pain and fury.

We learn what is holy and how to have reverence for it from a woman for whom nothing seems to be holy and who disrespectfully enters the sanctuary that was forbidden ground to her. It is rather like looking in Thecla's footsteps for a future for the Dominican religious life. And it seems appropriate for the Dominican movement, which since 1297 has had Mary Magdalene as its patron saint. For the second-century texts regularly mention conflicts between Mary of Magdala and Peter, and we can suppose that they reflect the discussion between those who regarded themselves as their successors. Already in early Christian writings Mary Magdalene, who after her personal encounter with Jesus spread the word that he had risen from the dead and was alive again, and who therefore is called the 'apostle of the apostles' (*apostola apostolorum*), is set against Peter, who as the chief among the apostles points out that it is his task to lead the church. For example, one text relates how

Peter sarcastically asks whether Jesus perhaps spoke to Mary Magdalene apart from his male disciples: 'Must we all turn and listen to her?' In his eyes that is evidently unimaginable. But that is precisely what a Dominican spirituality calls for: to turn to the constantly unexpected places where the God of salvation becomes visible and audible.

The Dominican mystic Catherine of Siena speaks with a passion which directly picks up the story of grandmother Teresa and which during her lifetime indeed converted people to listen to her preaching, including bishops and even the pope. Catherine recorded a vision in which the divine Wisdom in the form of the risen Christ urged her never to stop calling for grace for the world. For, the explanation is, God's Wisdom itself is the cause of that longing and God himself is the creator of the voice which calls for him. According to the divine Wisdom as Catherine sees him it is in the lamentation and crying of creatures that God shows his involvement in the world, her compassion for it – she uses the word *misericordia*, which means both mercy and compassion.

> Never let your will flag in asking me for help, and never stop calling on me to have mercy on the world . . . And bewail with a restless heart the death of this child, humankind, which you see in such a wretched state that your tongue cannot express it.

Have compassion on humankind, be bound up with specific people and indignant about what happens to them, separately and together, just as I, your God, who am involved, am bound up in compassion with them. And express your involvement, your indignation and the way in which you are moved with passion, like me, the Passionate One.

The touched body, the broken heart

Throughout the Dominican tradition God is first and foremost a God of salvation, a *Deus salutaris*. This applies in a particular way to Catherine: the idea and the experience of God's nearness, God's involvement and God's compassion are central to her spirituality. This spirituality certainly does not move Catherine of Siena only in the spirit. What she learns and thinks and what she says about it, concerns her physically. And it is precisely here that this woman, the official patron saint of lay Dominicans and since 1970 recognized in the Catholic Church by the highest authorities as a theologian with great authority – 'church teacher' – can still be a guide in our time.

Catherine was born in 1347 into the very large family of the weaver Jacopo Benincasa in Lapa di Puccio Piagenti. The family lived in reasonable prosperity, but had no political or social influence. She did not learn to read until the age of 16 or 17, and she could write only with great difficulty. At a very early stage she had an intense contact with death: her twin sister died soon after her birth and her sister Bonaventura, who was like a mother to her, died when Catherine was 15. From her early youth on, Catherine seemed opposed to the kind of life thought desirable for a woman in her milieu. She refused to marry and kept well away from anything that seemed to be the preparation for a marriage. In 1363, i.e. when she was around 16, she joined the so-called 'mantellata', a group of laywomen associated with the Dominican movement who did not marry – most of them were widows – and led a religious life in their own homes. After a period of almost complete separation she went out into the world. She looked after the sick and poor, but also spoke. A group came into being, a 'family' of disciples and friends of whom she was the spiritual centre, the 'Caterinati'. When she died of exhaustion in 1380 she had played a prominent political role in Italian society and in the church. She reminded church leaders in particular with striking boldness of what she thought were the responsibilities and tasks of their office.

At the decisive moments in her life Catherine of Siena was guided by visions and mystical experiences. In her religious life she was strongly orientated on following the suffering of Jesus Christ. In her later years she lived almost literally on the eucharist alone and there was every indication that she was in fact starving herself to death. In this respect she is not to be followed by people of our day, and we should not want to try to imitate her here in any way.

However, it is striking how everything in her religious sense turns on the heart and the body, her own and that of others. Thus there is a story of how when looking after a sick person she overcame her abhorrence and disgust at his body by drinking from the bowl in which the pus from his wound was collected. It seems wrong to dismiss this as a sign of masochism on her part. I see the gesture as an expression of fundamental solidarity and of being touched by the fate of another person. It shows that Catherine broke with the fundamental human tendency to stand apart from the bitter fate of others, and that she literally felt the bitterness of the fate of those whom she was looking after as her bitterness. With this gesture she honoured the other, not despite his sickness, weakness and vulnerability, but in it.

For Catherine, the heart is not exclusively the place of emotion. The heart is the place where we all stand face to face with ourselves and our own lives, the place of what she calls 'the cell of self-knowledge'. 'Create a pure heart within me' is the prayer in Psalm 51.12, 'make me new'. Catherine's life focused on getting such a 'pure' heart, a heart which has a divine quality in the way in which it is receptive and open to what happens. In just the same way, according to tradition the heart of Jesus of Nazareth is the centre and sum of his life in compassion, of the way in which he was touched and moved.

Life as the place of divine presence

By the way in which Catherine led her life, this life became a place of divine presence. She participated in the core of God and God in her. In the imagery of her visions she sees this as drinking from the heart of Jesus, as a baby drinks from its mother's breast, or as the implanting of her heart in Jesus' side and the implanting of Jesus' heart in her side. These are strange images for people today, but their message remains an urgent one. They depict the belief that the divine Spirit makes its presence felt in Catherine, and in people in general, in their abhorrence of what is not good and their indignation at what goes wrong, in their longing for a world in which people are no longer victims and in their sorrow at moments that they do not succeed:

> Who other than me has made you sad? . . . The battle is not going your way, but trust in my power and win the victory.

This is what Jesus says to Catherine in another vision, when she feels sombre and does not experience any glimpse of the divine presence. Her longing and steadfastness is reflected in God's obstinate concern for human salvation. That people are knocked sideways by what happens to themselves and others, that their hearts sometimes sink into their boots, indeed that they no longer have the heart to help – Catherine's biographer also relates a vision in which her heart is taken away, in which she says that as far as she knows she no longer has a heart – these are in a paradoxical way signs of hope.

I think of the statue by Ossip Zadkine (1890-1967) which commemorates the bombardment of the heart of the city of Rotterdam in May 1940. It is a human figure with its hands held up beseechingly and at the same time in self-defence, and with a great gap where the heart should be. To be so unreservedly desperate – 'You have deprived me of friends and companions, and all that I know is the dark,' says Psalm 88.19 – is a sign of hope. To refuse to forget terrors and to trivialize pain is to take them seriously and in so doing to bear witness that they deserve to be taken seriously. The obstinate complaint proclaims that the longing for another life which is really good, which is hidden in the heart of the pain, deserves to be taken seriously. In men and women the heart that is moved to compassion and thus no longer knows where it can rest is a sanctuary of the God of salvation and liberation, the *Deus salutaris* who is central to Dominican spirituality. It is a sanctuary where God is present as a deprivation, a passionate longing that knows at the very depth that it is not in vain because it is seen and heard.

Compassion with pain and involvement with desire are therefore perhaps the signs *par excellence* of divine presence. To be moved and shocked at what happens to people and what this does to them is a way of perceiving God's presence. Compassion is contemplation in the Dominican sense. Precisely for that reason Dominican spirituality is at its deepest level a lay spirituality. ✝

Catherine of Siena had to overcome inevitable resistance to arrive at the insight that as a lay person she was called on to embody the Dominican tradition. According to her biographer, Catherine was told in a vision by Jesus Christ himself to get out of the confines of her house and walk fully in the footsteps of Dominic. He 'founded his Order in the first instance for people to be helped', and that is what she too now had to go and do. Expressing the prejudices of her contemporaries, Catherine objected that she was 'the frailest of all' and a 'poor creature'. She pointed out that she was a woman, that men looked down on women and that it went against good manners for women and men to treat each other as equals. Thereupon Jesus replied to her in her vision:

> Am I not he who created humankind, men and women? Can I not give
> the grace of my spirit to whom I will? For me there is neither man nor

woman, commoner nor nobleman; all are alike to me.

Catherine is a lay person in every sense of the word. She has no office in the church, no political power, no social pretensions, no social role and no specific skill or systematic schooling. And none of that need change. In her spiritual world God is not an authority outside her nor is Jesus Christ an exalted symbol that must be venerated in the way prescribed by the church, or a model outside her, accessible only through the correct reading of old texts. He is the image of God's compassion, a compassion which according to the words of the best known Dominican mystic, Meister Eckhart, needs to be born in her own soul. From a Dominican perspective the important thing is evidently not to give form to one's own life in accordance with the traditional guidelines of the church. One's own existence, one's own body and one's own heart must be transformed into a dwelling place of the divine compassion.

God in all, all in God

It is clear to anyone who reads Catherine's writings that in her experience Dominican spirituality does not mean any segregation. For her, God is a word for Someone who – Something that – is encountered in the midst of movement and the unrest of life. Her God is intimately interwoven with life and is ultimately inaccessible apart from it. In the preface to the book in which she presents her spirituality and her theological views, her *Dialogue with Divine Providence*, Catherine depicts herself as someone who in the midst of all kinds of activity tries to discover the true significance of events:

> A soul rises up, restless with tremendous desire for God's honour and the salvation of souls. She has for some time exercised herself in virtue and has become accustomed to dwelling in the cell of self-knowledge in order to know better God's goodness toward her, since upon knowledge follows love. And loving, she seeks to pursue truth and clothe herself in it.

For Catherine, to know God is to see the countless forms and moments 'with the eyes of a living soul' (see the previous chapter) and to know that goodness, involvement and compassion manifest themselves in one's life and in the lives of the others with whom one is bound up. In her view, only when one really knows these moments and at the same time is aware that the word 'God' points to these moments, that God is present in them, can one love God: 'knowledge is followed by love'.

Dominican spirituality is to live in the love of God in this sense. In other words, it is to live with a passion for the good which comes to light in life and longing, passion and striving, hope and despair, and also – though Catherine did not have much of an eye for this – in laughter and enjoyment of the company of others. We are bound up with all these facets because our life is bound up with the lives of others and what happens in them. 'God' is a word that denotes the conviction that our own lives, the lives of others and reality generally are held together and supported at the deepest level by this goodness. In a sense this conviction changes our view of everything but in this new view there is room for our whole life in all its facets, whether everyday or exalted. Catherine's biographer Raymond of Capua paints a picture which is too attractive not to quote in full.

> The one who dives into the sea and swims under water sees nothing and touches nothing except for the seawater and the things that are in the water. If things from outside fall into the water, the diver sees them, but only in the water and as they look in the water. So too the soul which is totally immersed in God is transformed, so that all its thoughts, its understanding, its love and its memory are taken up into God and are concerned only with God. It sees itself and the other only in God; it thinks of others and of itself exclusively in God.

God is seen as a place in which everyone has a space, but in which the appearance of everything changes, because the spaces differ and different light falls on things. Everything becomes visible at the deepest level as supported by, surrounded with and steeped in an all-pervading, all-permeating compassion which is present everywhere.

Thus to live in the world 'in God' and to experience the world 'in God' is at the same time to be sent into the world. To see that the world is borne up by compassion and to love this compassion is at the same time to be given the task of living by compassion and embodying it.

To perceive all that exists, everything in one's own life and that of others 'in God' means that everyday things are taken out of the sphere of the obvious, the unimportant that is not worth attention and the trivial that needs to be denied. The feminist theologian Ina Praetorius speaks in this connection of 'de-trivialization'. The things that can be regarded as obvious, not worth paying attention to and too ordinary to give another thought to are often those things which are central in human life. Conversations in the staff canteen, when cooking and washing up, or in talk shows on the television are an expression of the concern which people have for themselves and for each other; in them it becomes evident how carefully they try to cope with their own needs and longings and those of others, how dedicated they are to the people around them. The inventiveness which people show in order to live decently in the midst of everything that happens to them and to help others to live decently, the confusion and the sorrow that this causes, the difficulty and the pain that it brings – these things are thought unimportant in our culture. So-called 'reality TV' shows what is thought to be exciting: people behaving as hunters always in search of a new thrill, as seekers constantly concerned with their own interest who exploit others to achieve their ends. Here the common opinion is that worries like how to get by on one's income, how to deal with a father who hasn't recognized anyone for years, what it means to be married in a situation in which one is alienated from one's partner, all these things which affect the life of many people to a considerable degree, are uninteresting.

That is bad, and damages our society. At the same time it is striking how little consideration there is in practice of what is important and what is not. There are an enormous number of organizations and volunteers who in the midst of our harsh and sometimes unfeeling society try to be a seeing eye, a listening ear or a compassionate heart for those in need. They lend a listening ear to what people want to say in their own homes, in the street or in the coffee bar, or offer people the opportunity to share their difficulties and their sorrow with others on the telephone. They take neighbours, members of the family or those who live in the local centre for asylum-seekers to places that they cannot get to by themselves, carry on conversations with authorities for those who are not really capable of doing it for themselves, organize street parties, or support the families of the terminally ill who would like to die at home.

In short, those who are able to disregard the greyness of everyday life and catch sight of what is really taking place in it see that Dominic has countless followers. They themselves would not normally put it this way, but the God of salvation is sought by many, and numerous people work for the salvation of souls which are in danger of getting lost. In particular, countless women still follow the footsteps of Catherine of Siena without knowing it: they give their hearts to those who are in need. Those who succeed in doing this continue to believe that these things are not banal or unimportant or trivial; they can discover the extent to which compassion is a cement in our society which usually remains invisible. They can learn to see that they themselves live by compassion and can come to realize that a commitment to compassion is really a matter of life and death.

Contemplata aliis tradere

However, none of this is by any means obvious. The forces of banalization and trivialization are strong. 'Volunteer work' is often regarded as virtually insignificant or ineffective, even by those who devote themselves to it. And even an acute thinker like the Dominican Thomas Aquinas, who has already been mentioned, does not seem to see fully the divine quality of everyday compassion, which is the point on which the Dominican spirituality of Catherine of Siena always turns.

More perhaps than any other theologian, Thomas tries to disclose the reality in which we live as a place of divine presence. He tries to speak of God as the One who reveals himself in reality, as the One from Whom all things come, in Whom all things consist and to Whom all things go. For Thomas, God is the One in whom we live, move and have our being, as the apostle Paul says with the Greek poets in the Acts of the Apostles (17.28): believing is living in reality as the room of God. But then it becomes evident that in the end Thomas takes seriously only the knowledge of God in words and concepts and scarcely has any eye for doing practical justice to the divine Presence in life in the midst of reality. A sentence which is famous in Dominican circles comes from Thomas: 'Just as it is better to give light than only to have the light (oneself), so it is also better to hand on the things that one has contemplated than just to contemplate them: *majus est contemplata aliis tradere quam solum contemplari.*' And in his view Dominican life involves handing down the things that one has discovered in contemplating God. But here Thomas seems to make a sharp distinction between 'external activities like almsgiving, offering hospitality to strangers and such things', and emphatically applying oneself to what he calls the 'fullness of contemplation'. According to Thomas the fullness of contemplation ultimately takes place in studying the writings of the Bible, the church tradition and the texts of great thinkers. In his eyes this fullness needs to be communicated to others in sermons in the strict sense, or in the giving of theological instruction. For him these are the most exalted activities, because they communicate know-ledge of the most exalted mysteries.

Here Thomas displays a remarkable blind spot. Everyday concerns, which keep everyone including himself alive, seem to lie outside his field of vision; the money on which he lives is collected, the books and the papers that he uses are made, his food is cooked and his bedchamber is prepared. He does not see himself as a layman but as a specialist, who thinks that his own speciality is the most important of all. Theologians and church officials, and also scientists and professional thinkers, still act like this regularly and thus create a gulf between themselves and what is taking place in human life at an everyday level, even in their own lives. In the end, Thomas cannot think of handing on the things of God that one has appropriated through contemplation – *contemplata aliis tradere* – other than as a transmission of the specialist knowledge that has been acquired by study.

Things are totally different in the Dominican lay spirituality of Catherine of Siena. Catherine would regard contemplation as remaining in the cell of self-knowledge in the midst of everyday life, as learning to know the divine compassion better while one receives food and care from others and gives alms and offers hospitality to strangers.

Thus to make efforts to welcome abused women or the homeless can be seen as a form of self-knowledge in God, of knowledge of God in oneself. We can be practical forms of the knowledge that we live by virtue of the fact that we were welcomed when it was necessary. This can express the certainty that the world has been created as a space in which everyone can and may exist, the certainty that where people long for this place, God's presence shows itself. In short, it can be a form of Dominican spirituality. Contemplating God and handing on to others what has dawned on us – *contemplari* and *contemplata aliis tradere* – then run smoothly into each other. They are then in fact two sides of the same coin, true knowledge of the divine compassion. Along these lines, for me a truly Dominican theology is a theology which can find words for the God who has come into view in this way, a theology which can speak about what it means to live with the world in this God and to live with this God in the world.

Against cynicism as a god

Dominican spirituality is a matter of keeping watch in partnership with the divine compassion. It is a matter of perceiving the presence of the *Deus salutaris*, the God who is salvation and liberation, a presence which supports and comforts, activates and disturbs; a presence which usually remains hidden in indifference. And it is to embody and inspire a caring and motivating power that can combat the cynical view that all this will not lead anywhere. It is to make use of what the present Master of the Dominican Order, Timothy Radcliffe, calls the freedom not to escape, in body or spirit, but really to belong to the situation and to what happens to people in it, what they desire and how they try to keep themselves and others alive.

In our society, which has no dogmas and no prevailing religion, one could say that cynical indifference is the all-pervasive idolatry. In this 'splintered time, when cynicism is god', Dominican spirituality embodies a 'possible heresy', as the Nigerian British writer Ben Okri puts it. The heresy to be found here is to dare to be truly religious. Okri writes:

> To be truly religious does not require an institution, it requires terror, faith, compassion, imagination and a belief in more than three dimensions. It also requires love.

This is a love which consists in being able to be touched and from there to feel, to speak and to act. (It consists in letting the heart be moved, losing it, to have it changed and get it back again, as happened with Catherine.) It is a love which ensures that we burst out in fury at what happens, as did grandmother Teresa. In this way the possibility arises of our finding new and surprising forms of remaining faithful to God's holiness.

4

Like an Antenna: Dominican life as constant prayer

When as a working mother with a young baby she finally had a few free moments, the Jewish writer Judy Petsonk was struck by the impossibility of choosing between the different opportunities that she now had. Should she fold up the washing? If she did, she wouldn't have to do it later. Should she begin to do some gymnastic exercises? She hadn't done any for ages. Or should she open her prayer book again? She had left it aside for a long time. She writes how finally she got the happy inspiration of doing everything at the same time.

> I ran inside, grabbed a prayer book, scurried back outside, wrapped myself in a sheet, said the blessing for putting on a prayer shawl, and felt the Presence gently embracing me with arms of sunlight. I danced around the yard, folding the laundry in great swooping dancerly motions, turning pages as I passed the prayerbook perched on a lawn garden chair, singing, laughing at myself. I could feel the Presence bathe me in Her loving laughter.

In the subtitle of the chapter which includes these sentences, Petsonk writes that in this way she found God in a pile of laundry, 'which sounds like a comedown from Sinai', the holy mountain of God's Presence, 'but isn't'. On the contrary, what she describes is precisely what the Psalms call entering 'the sanctuary', 'the forecourt' or 'the temple gate'. It is entering the space of prayer. At least, of prayer as it must be written about in an exploration of Dominican spirituality.

Prayer is a difficult subject to talk about and write about. It is certainly also a difficult subject to read about. I don't get very far with what most people write about prayer. All kinds of misunderstandings arise over prayer, like the notion that it is a matter of uttering particular formulae which of themselves guarantee contact with God. Or – and in a sense this is the opposite – the misunderstanding is that prayer is something special and extraordinary, a contact between the soul in its unfathomable, almost unattainable depths and God in his immeasurable exaltation. Then praying becomes something that lies completely outside the usual categories of doing and thinking, seeing and feeling.

So I hesitate to say anything about prayer. But there is no avoiding the fact that a book which sets out to explore the possibilities of living our daily existence in a Dominican sense also has to contain a chapter about prayer. From of old praying has been regarded as an essential part of the religious life. Judy Petsonk sheds a new light on a call which resounds in the psalms to the whole earth to sing to God, to rejoice before him and to honour him. She suggests that prayer means that everything – the whole creation and the whole of life, from the most exalted thoughts and the highest searchings of the soul to doing the shopping or folding up the laundry – is brought into the sphere of the divine Presence. 'Enter the gates and give thanks, go within the court and praise, praise the holy name,' Psalm 100 calls out to all that exists. Petsonk tells of a moment when in her experience this in fact takes place. And she suggests that here the traditional formulae of prayer, which are drawn from the Psalms and from the rest of the biblical and post-biblical traditions, can be a support. Celebrating the liturgy and saying prayers, taking old or new words on to one's lips and making stylized or spontaneous gestures – all this can help to articulate the desire for divine Presence and the true experience of it. They recall that this Presence has brought us forth and that we belong to it, to paraphrase Psalm 100 once again. So they invite us to go and stand in the space which gives us this feeling.

Not collecting water, but thirst

In a book in which he wanted to help the first Dominicans to become good preachers, Humbert of Romans quotes with approval Bernard of Clairvaux (c.1090-1153), who in his time was regarded as a great authority on preaching. Bernard does not want to have anything to do with people who, out of what in his eyes is a false concern for others, open their mouths all too quickly and begin to preach. He says of them that they 'pour themselves out before they are full'. Humbert takes over Bernard's advice: those with understanding make themselves bowls and first allow themselves to be filled with spiritual knowledge. Then, out of the abundance that he gets in this way – Humbert has only male preachers in view – the preacher pours out again the living water that he has received. According to Humbert it is not good to be a pipe with water being poured in at one end and running almost straight out at the other. In his view it is with good reason that the New Testament tells how the disciples of Jesus were first filled with the Holy Spirit and only then began to preach (Acts 2.4).

It seems obvious that you can't give until you have, even in the spiritual sphere. You can never hand on to others knowledge of spiritual matters that you yourself do not possess. But I think that the water pipe is a more adequate image for the Dominican spirituality which I am trying to explore in these pages than the bowl. It is not a question of filling oneself with academic knowledge or deep experiences and then sharing out this fullness. It is more Dominican to make oneself spiritually empty, or better to *realize* that one is spiritually empty. We have to allow ourselves to realize how much we long for a clarifying thought, how necessary a truly liberating word really is for us. For that to be possible, faith is required, trust that a soul which really realizes how necessary it is to say something sensible and to do something good will get what it needs to do so. A pipe from which no water flows cannot receive any new water either; a pipe from which water flows as it were sucks up new water. Or, to abandon metaphors, those who are silent are not focused on new wholesome insights with which to comfort, to encourage others and themselves and to help them to discover a meaningful life. By contrast, those who speak are constantly compelled to search for what can be said. Thus speaking itself becomes a prayer for words that can be spoken and action becomes a call for insight into what has to be done to make God's kind of freedom and peace present.

Those who are bound up with others stand with them before God with their questions. There is an image of this in the Dominican tradition, which the Dominican writer Jean de Mailly recorded in 1243 like this:

Dominic, knowing that seed bears fruit when it is scattered but goes bad when it is hoarded, no longer wanted all his brethren to remain in one place. So he called them together and said that he wanted to scatter them all to different places, even though they were still a very small number.

It is not a matter of becoming a big, strong plant. One has to have the courage to be a seed among the other seeds, borne up by the trust that all this seed is made in order to grow and that it will result in a garden full of flowers. 'Joyfully you will draw water from the springs of salvation,' says the prophet Isaiah (12.3). Dominican spirituality is a matter of living by this biblical promise.

For those who utterly trust this promise and make their own existence dependent on it, it also becomes a personal problem when the flowers fail to materialize and the seed threatens to be choked in the earth. 'I stretch out my hands to you, my heart like a land thirsty,' says Psalm 143.6. According to tradition, Dominic prayed this verse with special devotion. And that prayer is the heart of the life of those who follow in his footsteps. It is not by collecting water but by giving ourselves without reserve to the thirst that we share with others, to the longing that people have in common with one another, that we know what we must do and say.

In all things longing for a fulfilled life

That Dominic prayed Psalm 143 passionately is related in a little book entitled *The Nine Ways of Prayer of St Dominic*. The text dates from soon after 1260 and according to the experts is based on historical information about Dominic's life and person which came to light in the process of his canonization. But what I think makes this little book worth reading is not the historical information that it contains. It can be read as a reflection on the Dominican life, seen as a form of constant prayer. Dominic in this book is the one who embodies and gathers together this life.

Ignatius of Loyola (1491–1556), the founder of the Jesuit Order, left his followers a little book of *Spiritual Exercises*. It describes for the readers a method of taking part in important episodes of the history of God with humankind as this has been preserved in the Christian tradition, and especially the history of Jesus Christ as the Gospels relate it. The purpose is that readers should identify with this history by imagining scenes from it so intensely – seeing it, feeling it, hearing it and smelling it – that in a sense these scenes become more real than events in their own existence. Since they were composed, Ignatius' *Spiritual Exercises* have had an enormous influence on the spirituality and the prayer life of Catholics. For centuries the message has been that it is necessary to stand aside from the events in one's own life, and that true certainty and true direction can be found only in an exclusive concentration on the treasury of Christian faith. Like Ignatius' *Spiritual Exercises*, *The Nine Ways of Prayer of St Dominic* is a concentrated view of the life of the believer, written down so that posterity could adopt it. However, the spirituality that is expressed in the two writings differs notably.

The little book about Dominic's ways of prayer is far less well known than Ignatius' *Exercises*. Paradoxically enough, the reason for this is also connected with what seems to be the most important quality of the work. Ignatius develops a detailed method. He orders people to separate themselves as far as possible 'from all friends and acquaintances and from all earthly cares' so that 'the more our soul separates itself in solitude', the more it is in a position to come close to God. In this way it makes itself receptive 'to the gifts and graces of the divine and supreme goodness'. A number of carefully described steps in this isolation lead to the desired encounter with God. However, the unknown author of *The Nine Ways of Prayer of St Dominic* does not describe any worked-out method. He presents Dominic as the attractive example of a man who in the midst of an everyday life full of cares is focused on God. His aim is not for people to be helped in isolation to discover what God's will is and then to submit themselves to this will for the rest of their lives. The central question is how travelling and staying put, thinking, reading and speaking can in themselves become ways of desiring the fulfilled life in the space of God's presence as it is proclaimed by the biblical writings. Dominic is portrayed as someone who is in a position to do this in an exemplary manner.

A good attitude in the midst of everything

Now let's turn our attention to what *The Nine Ways of Prayer of St Dominic* says about life as a constant prayer in the Dominican sense. For through all the time-conditioned forms a spirituality comes to light which can still have meaning.

It is said that on his many journeys Dominic regularly parted company with his travelling companions to go on ahead or, more often, to remain far behind. According to the New Testament, at the end of a day full of activities Jesus went into the mountains to pray alone. In the book about his ways of prayer, what Dominic did is connected with this. However, according to the author, Dominic evidently found the necessary solitude in himself, in the midst of everyday life. At some distance from his travelling companions he concentrated on what kept his soul active and gave the holy fire that burned deep within him, as in others, the opportunity to blaze. Those who at some point do not talk to fellow-travellers in the train, on a bicycle, in a car or during a walk because they are sunk in thought about what they have heard or what they must say or do next will be surprised by the everyday nature of this summit of Dominican life.

For that is what it is, according to the little book about Dominic's ways of prayer:

> The brethren thought that in this kind of prayer the saint acquired the fullness of sacred scripture and the very heart of the understanding of God's words, and also a power and boldness to preach fervently, and a hidden intimacy with the Holy Spirit to know hidden things.

One reason why the author emphasizes the ease with which Dominic deals with the things of God is certainly that this is supposed to be a sign of his holiness. But it is significant that this holiness is seen in terms of what every preacher does in preparing a sermon and what every speaker does before she or he speaks. Even cherishing a small personal tic to help one concentrate is evidently not shameful in this connection: 'And a curious thing about this form of prayer was that he seemed to be brushing away ashes or flies from before his face.'

It is good here to remember that in the Middle Ages praying was usually closely connected with concentration. Printing had not yet been invented and texts were scarce and hard to come by. In a culture in which written texts are sparse and thought is above all based on memory, it requires a great deal of effort to call to mind all that one has heard or read on a particular subject, to order the knowledge in one's head and to get through to the essentials. For example, it is related of Thomas Aquinas that when he was writing – in fact dictating to scribes – a commentary on the letters of Paul he sometimes sent the secretaries away, fell to the ground and prayed until clarity was given him. Of course in our age of photocopiers, word processors and on-line libraries, the situation is fundamentally different. But the anecdote about Thomas reminds people today that the quest for understanding can itself be a form of prayer. Writing and working on a text at the computer, gathering and brainstorming about what must be done and how it can best be tackled, going around for a long time with a question or half a thought about some personal experience, tracing the meaning of a text with dedication or surfing on the Internet, are ultimately forms of prayer.

At least, that is the case if an attitude is adopted here which makes these activities so many attempts to gain insight into the situation, into one's own existence, into the traces of God which are illuminated in this way. *The Nine Ways of Prayer of St Dominic* suggests that it is literally a matter of attitude. In the introduction the writer lists a whole series of people who have written important things about prayer. However, a quite special form of prayer is central to his book, a form which makes productive use of the attitude of the body. 'So the soul, as it causes the body to move, is in turn moved by the body.' As the writer of the book about Dominic's ways of prayer imagines it, prayer evidently cannot be detached from the body, from the history in which the body is entangled, from the pain which attaches to it and from the joy that permeates it. The way in which the body stands in the world, the way in which its own situation is literally embodied and the way in which the body allows itself to be touched and moved by history brings the soul into contact with God. In the Dominican sense praying proves to be a question above all of finding a good attitude in the midst of all that is and all that happens.

Looking expectantly towards God

The words of the Psalms clearly function as a pointer in the discovery of this attitude. Psalm 40 sums up the whole Bible in the history of an individual.

> Expectantly I looked towards God,
> he pulled me up from the seething chasm,
> he set my feet on rock.
> You gave me an open ear,

then I said, 'Here I am, I am coming';
in the scroll of your book it is written:
my delight is to do your will.
I proclaim the message of your saving justice,
I do not hold my tongue.

Longing for salvation and experiencing it; the biblical writings read like a message of longing for salvation and the promise of it. Those who speak in them long for and proclaim salvation by living redemptively and speaking about it, as praise of the God who is this salvation.

All the books of the Bible tell in their own way of the presence of the God of salvation. The Christian tradition has always started from the fact that the deprivation, the desire, the trust and joy which are spoken of elsewhere in the Bible take on special intensity in the poems and prayers which are collected in the book of Psalms. The verses of the psalms express the soul of the biblical writings. Those who take them up, speak them and apply them to themselves let their own breath coincide with the breath which inspires the biblical texts and join in their spirit. Therefore time and again the recurrent prayer of the psalms has always been an important ingredient of religious life. For that reason too, above all, verses from the psalms are put on Dominic's lips in *The Nine Ways of Prayer of St Dominic*. As a canon in Osma he must have sung the psalms day by day in the liturgy. He was steeped in them. According to the author of the little book about his ways of prayer, his life as an itinerant preacher was not less in accord with the spirit of the psalms, but more. Now their sighings and outbursts set his body in motion and through the body moved the soul all the more urgently.

According to the New Testament, especially the letter to the Hebrews, Psalm 40 is fulfilled in particular in the life of Jesus of Nazareth. The heart of God's law is the heart of his existence (Hebrews 10.5-7). So in the book about his ways of prayer Dominic is characterized as someone who follows the history of Jesus in his body, by his bodily attitude, not by literally imitating Jesus, but by seeing his own life in the mirror of that of Jesus. Dominic sees that he is bowed down under the situation of the world as it is, and he literally bows down; he is oppressed by the sense of being trapped in this situation and throws himself flat on the ground; he is tormented by the knowledge that he and his associates, along with others, perpetuate this situation despite all their good intentions, and scourges himself; he senses that God has bowed down towards him, and bows in reverence before the images which try to express this mystery.

Just as Dominic does not imitate the Jesus of the Gospels, so too present-day people must not imitate Dominic as he is portrayed in the little book about his ways of prayer. His way of praying is no longer ours and must not become ours now; there are few people who would want to recommend flagellation as a form of prayer. But the close link which *The Nine Ways of Prayer of St Dominic* makes between prayer and the body remains valuable. Praying is perhaps in fact no more and no less than standing in such a way that your body expresses that in some way you are bowed down, and then raising yourself up in such a way that you realize through your body that you could hit yourself, and then acting in such a way that you feel that you can raise your head again. It is to move in such a way that it really becomes a living truth that the space in which you can live and what you can do is a wonderful gift and an unexpected present. As Psalm 67.7 says in all simplicity: 'The earth has yielded its produce; God, our God, has blessed us.' Each generation will have to find its own forms to help it really to live in the truth of this insight. Here the body time and again has to be transformed into an expression of hope and despair, into a form of disappointment and joy, into an incarnation of complaint and longing. In this way the body becomes the summary of human existence, the concentrated presence of one's own history and consequently a place of divine history. From a Dominican perspective prayer shapes human existence, just as at a particular time and at a particular place it takes concrete form to become a place where there is a prospect of a liberating word, a place where this word can find a hearing and make itself felt.

Constant prayer

According to the author of *The Nine Ways of Prayer of St Dominic*, Dominic was driven on by a longing like that of a thirsty person who comes to a spring or a traveller who at long last is approaching his home. On his way he prayed with Psalm 28, 'Do not be deaf to me. If you stay silent I shall be like those who sink into oblivion.' He kept on doing this until in fact a liberating word broke through to him. The depth of the longing opens the ear to words of salvation, sharpens the eye for traces of liberation and makes it impossible, once they have been heard and seen, not to hand them on to all those others who live with the same hunger as ours. It is not by shutting oneself off from everything else that receptivity to traces of God reaches its greatest, that prayer for the longed-for and promised breakthrough of liberation and salvation becomes strongest. On the contrary, prayer takes on its most authentic form in those who really allow the outreach for a good life, a fulfilled existence and a healed heart which is taking place all over the world to get through to them. Such people will automatically intensify the longing in their own soul to the utmost.

In the end Dominican life is constant prayer in this sense. Dominican life is an attempt to give form to the longing for liberation and salvation and a liberated life which according to Christian conviction come 'from God' and are divine. It is from here that the explicit prayer which to some degree is separated from the stream of daily life finally emerges, and it is to this that it is in turn directed. In *The Nine Ways of Prayer of St Dominic* we read that after praying with the community in the midst of which he lived, in the liturgy or at mealtimes, Dominic could take the atmosphere of devotion and concentration which prevailed there away with him. He could remain in it in order to come to himself and it helped him to put himself in the sphere of divine Presence.

In particular, seeking insight and truth through study put him in this context. In this way reading became the visible form of prayer *par excellence*. The author of *The Nine Ways of Prayer of St Dominic* gives a vivid description of how Dominic deeply and almost aloud entered into discussion with books as though he were disputing with a friend: at one moment he seemed impatient, at another he seemed to be listening quietly and with attention; then again he would wrestle with what was said before claiming that he was persuaded by it, laughing and weeping at the same time. Finally, he would rise respectfully and bow to the book as though he were thanking a very special person for favours bestowed. This story, too, bears traces of a time when books were precious and rare and in which an aura of authority and loftiness was attached to the written word. But those who have sought fanatically for information, or with a thumping heart have opened a book which has happened to come into their hands because it promises a long hoped-for clarification; those who angrily or sadly throw down a newspaper because of its contents; those who when surfing on the Internet stare intently at what they have found on the screen, know that Dominic's prayerful way of reading still exists. Prayer is still offered in the passionate search for truth; it is intensely longed for and reverently dealt with once it is found.

It is striking and significant for Dominican spirituality that *The Nine Ways of Prayer of St Dominic* calls studying and disputing with a book 'a beautiful form of praying, full of devotion and grace'. The quest for truth in general and study in particular have always enjoyed high esteem among Dominicans in connection with good and responsible preaching. The earliest constitutions already state that those who study must not lightly be hindered by being given other tasks. If need be they must have special facilities, like their own cell and their own lamp so that they can also work through the night. But when all is said and done, perhaps the way of prayer described as follows is even more typical of the Dominican spirit:

> Dominic was also often found stretching his whole body up towards heaven in prayer, like a choice arrow shot straight up from a bow. He had his hands stretched right up above his head, joined together or slightly open as if to catch something from heaven.

Here, if anywhere, it becomes clear that *The Nine Ways of Prayer of St Dominic* is not about specific pious practices, but about the stylized expression of the Dominican life itself. It discloses life itself as a form of prayer.

Life as an antenna

Religious life is always understood as an attempt to live radically in accordance with the so-called Beatitudes, which in the Gospel of Matthew form the beginning of what is called Jesus' Sermon on the Mount. The Dominican theologian Albert the Great (*c.*1200–80), Thomas Aquinas' teacher, saw the Sermon on the Mount as a whole as an introduction to the Dominican life. The Beatitudes sum up the starting points of that life as it were in advance:

> How blessed are the poor in spirit:
> the kingdom of Heaven is theirs.
> Blessed are the gentle:
> they shall have the earth as inheritance.

Blessed are those who mourn:
they shall be comforted.
Blessed are those who hunger and thirst for uprightness:
they shall have their fill.
Blessed are the merciful:
they shall have mercy shown them.
Blessed are the pure in heart:
they shall see God.
Blessed are the peacemakers:
they shall be recognized as children of God.
Blessed are those who are persecuted in the cause of uprightness:
the kingdom of heaven is theirs (Matthew 5.3-10).

This is the basic law of a life of longing, of being outstretched to God, or, as the text itself says, a life 'poor in spirit'.

By literally stretching himself out to heaven, according to the little book on his ways of prayer, Dominic

> won from God for himself and his brethren such delight and enjoyment in putting the Beatitudes into practice, that each would feel himself blessed in the most profound poverty, in bitter grief, in severe persecution, in great hunger and thirst for righteousness, in all the cares and worries of mercy, and that they would consider it a pleasure to observe the commandments with devotion and to follow the evangelical counsels.

They knew themselves blessed in poverty, grief, persecution, hunger and thirst. It seems that to stretch oneself out towards the divine Presence in this form of prayer at the same time means to come into contact with the Presence. The longing for, the expectation of God's kingdom of peace and justice are experienced as a form in which the fulfilment of this promise is present in a hidden but real way. Poverty can make one feel the lack of the true riches which give life, and in this way gives a precise view of this kingdom. Grief can be experienced as a longing for joy and thus as the presence of this joy in a negative form, as presence in the form of absence and deprivation. Those who are persecuted are bound up with the righteousness which in human history is hunted down and persecuted time and again, and those who with care and concern try to live with compassion for others experience in the difficulties that this causes the negative side of the happiness that emerges, even if something of the longed-for happiness is also realized.

So, blessed are the poor in spirit. In my view, something comes

to light here of the ultimate mystery of religious life, in any case of
the Dominican form of it. According to the tradition of the
Christian religious life, the true life is found only by those who
voluntarily follow in the footsteps of Jesus and his first disciples, who
went around with no possessions and no security. The choice of
poverty and insecurity is an expression of the conviction that the
gospel of salvation and liberation is not addressed to those who live
in security and safety, but to those who can only hope for a decent
life for themselves and others. The 'poverty of spirit' with which
Dominicans are concerned consists in the choice to share their
uncertainty. This amounts to leaving aside the struggle for the
security which is attainable for some here and now, deliberately not
seizing the opportunities which present themselves for achieving
security. It means deliberately and passionately continuing to wait,
to hope for the life that can be called completely good because it is
good for all people. 'Poverty of spirit' is the option for a life which
has the form of a prayer. It is a matter of possessing nothing, or as
little as possible. It is a matter of in fact daring to be dependent on
the good that can only happen to people, that can only be given:
quite unexpectedly or as the always surprising fruit of hard effort.
And so it is a matter of being ready to be oppressed if the good fails
to materialize and in the light of this experience to point to what is
lacking, to lament it and do something about it. It is a matter of
being modest and decisive at the same time.

The person who wrote *The Nine Ways of Prayer of St Dominic*
cannot possibly have had such an idea, but as a present-day reader,
when reading about Dominic's open, receptive attitude I think of an
antenna. To live the Dominican life is to live as an antenna. It is to
live in a receptive openness which is dependent on the signals of
divine salvation and true life that are offered to us. The antenna is
not the important thing, for the antenna cannot itself call to life the
signal from which it derives its right to exist. The important thing is
what the antenna receives. To live the Dominican life is to live a life
that is completely focused on receiving traces of the God of salvation
as well as possible and amplifying them as clearly as possible.

A mendicant order

According to a well-known legend, Dominic's mother had a dream
before he was born, in which a dog with a burning torch in its

mouth ran through the world. It set everything alight. Dominic is often depicted with this dog, and the dog has become an image of the Dominicans who as the 'hounds of God' – *domini canes* – were to set the world alight with their fire. In my view, setting fire to the whole world is a quite violent image and I cannot help feeling that in her dream Dominic's mother already saw something of the fanaticism with which over the course of history Dominicans pursued supposed heretics and burned those who were thought to be witches.

However, sometimes the picture of the dog with a torch is unintentionally developed in a way which fits better with what we have seen in these chapters to be the core of Dominican spirituality. It is probably unintentional, but in some portrayals the dog with a torch in its mouth seems to show no sign of running into the world and spreading the fire. It seems, rather, to be offering this torch to Dominic. And I think that that is an attractive symbol. The gist of this book is that Dominicans find the fire by which they live in the world in which they live. They kindle their light at the places where the fire of the divine Spirit burns, resounds in true words and becomes visible in actions which further the true life. Certainly, the Dominican mission is a mission to speak and act, but for that to be possible it is a mission to listen to what is to be said and to see what is to be done. Dominican spirituality as it is portrayed here is not about going on one's way firmly convinced what life bound up with God in the footsteps of Jesus of Nazareth truly is. Dominican life is a life which knows itself to be sent to the places where people seek such a life in the space of God's wholesome presence, and where they already discover fragments of this as they seek. Before being a mission to give, the Dominican mission is a mission to receive. Before being a mission to kindle, the Dominican mission is a mission to be kindled.

Thus Dominican spirituality can never be other than an exploration, a form of truly seeking for true life. I feel that this is the deepest significance of the fact that the Dominican Order is a 'mendicant order', as it came to be called in history, an order of beggars. 'Take nothing with you' is the message that Dominic and his followers read in the Gospel of Matthew, as we saw in chapter 2. Do not get any riches for yourself and do not make yourself dependent on what you think you have or must have. Live by what comes your way and what you pick up: food and drink, housing and clothing, but also – and perhaps above all – salvation and goodness, traces of God and divine inspiration. Perhaps, given the black pages in the Dominican past, for Dominicans an addition should be made to the admonitions of the Gospel of Matthew not to take any gold or silver, or money, or purse for the journey, not to wear two garments, not to have either sandals or stick (Matthew 10.9-10): 'Don't take any burning torch with you.' Don't be seduced into the notion that fire burns in you and nowhere else. Watch and stay where you are until the hidden fire of the divine Spirit flares up, and kindle your own flame by that. Learn there what you must say, and discover what you have to do.

We can live our lives, arrange them and order them in such a way that they become a prayer, that everything is focused on hearing the words which bear witness to a divine truth and seeing the goodness in which the holy dwells. It is a basic Dominican conviction that this is possible. There is great pressure on this faith in a culture which is focused on getting things done and in a church climate dominated by the desire to control. But in this situation it is all the more urgent to show that we can live without declaring things to be possessions. We can live in dependence on the traces of the divine Presence which constantly shine out anew, in a constantly renewed trust in the space of the God of creation which opens up time and again. Anyone who has eyes to see can see everywhere a deep longing for such a life of grace. This imposes on Dominicans the task to explore what such a life could actually look like.

5

A Stranger on Earth: Life as a restless quest

A collection of short stories by the travel writer Bruce Chatwin was published under the title *Anatomy of Restlessness*. That would be a good description, perhaps not of the Dominican history as a whole but of the Dominican history at its best moments. Chatwin contrasts what he calls the 'nomadic initiative' with a civilization which orders reality in a fixed way and knows precisely what is important and good and what is not. By this he means the resolve to go away, literally or only in the spirit. The nomadic initiative is to take the decision, free from what is regarded as order, to go in search of what is really important and truly good.

It is quite clear from the story told by Jean de Mailly in the previous chapter and from the whole of its early history that the Dominican movement is indeed meant to be a *movement*. The central activity of Dominicans is described as 'itinerant preaching'. In short, at the origin of the religious life in the Dominican sense lies a nomadic initiative. Dominican life is not focused on a stable abode, but on wandering around. It is focused on finding places where truth and goodness shine through. In spiritual terms that ultimately means that it is about a questing existence that comes to rest only when it has found a place where life – time and again, always unexpectedly, always temporarily – takes on a divine quality.

Contemplation in the midst of movement

Now in our over-mobile world – chaotic and polluted by the constant movement of people and things – restlessness is not intrinsically a positive quality. Anyone who sees our stress and rush and the traffic jams which block our roads will tend, rather, to think that Blaise Pascal was right. Pascal wrote as early as the seventeenth century that human unhappiness is caused by our inability to remain quietly at home. According to him, movement and the constant change of views and prospects, of thoughts and fashions, distracts us from the rest which we so desperately need if we are really to come into contact with our own souls. In his view, the modern culture which was arising in his time was driven on by the need for something constantly new or surprising, for one new excitement after another. What we perceive around us, on our televisions and in ourselves, seems to prove him overwhelmingly right. At the beginning of the twenty-first century, shouldn't we turn away from the constant mobilization of everything and everyone? Shouldn't we make an effort to return to calmness, to stillness and concentration, to silence? Many spiritual people and movements are indeed concerned to do that.

According to the Dominican tradition, it is also important to stand aside from the tumult and the distraction, to stay silent and concentrate in the 'cell of self-knowledge', in order to find our own souls and to experience what is revealed in them. But from a Dominican perspective this can never end up in a life within an enclosed world of calm and silence, a secure dwelling place which shuts out all threats. I can only express it in a paradox. Dominican spirituality – and thus also the Dominican quest for rest and silence – involves mobility *vis-à-vis* all things, even *vis-à-vis* the very mobility which is so prevalent in our time. Those who feel driven and insecure because everything in our society and in their personal life is being turned upside down are challenged by the Dominican tradition to seek not less but, in a sense, more movement. In other words, their own nomadic initiative remains important. For from a Dominican point of view it is not enough to be mobile in the footsteps of our culture, which regards dynamic growth and progress as the supreme values. The important thing is to be as mobile as possible also with respect to this culture.

A life outside the chaotic turbulence of our time cannot save us. The only wholesome course, as a sign of the presence of the God of salvation, is to be really attentive in the midst of this turbulence which surrounds us, permeates us and drags us along. Mobility, whether we choose it ourselves or it is imposed upon us, remains extremely important. It detaches people from the position which they once occupied or in which they found themselves through circumstances, from views which have been handed down to them or which they have chosen. It forces them constantly to reconsider choices or decisions. Thus mobility is essential. But there is a need for attentiveness in the midst of this mobility to ensure that not every moment proves principally to be a transition to the next moment, that value is not attached exclusively to objects as representing the beginning of capital to be acquired, and that the significance of an experience is not seen in its sensational character. The mobility that characterizes our existence in today's world ensures that things constantly appear in another light. Attentiveness ensures that in the midst of these changes we really perceive moments, experiences and things, see them in their own worth and significance. If we do, they prove to be figures of the holy, traces of the Holy One. Such attentiveness, such dedication, finds places in which to be at home, in the midst of constant change and uprooting. Those are the places of true repose.

As a stranger

Dominic did not talk during his lifetime about attentiveness and dedication to what offers itself. He did not call his followers to this. He 'just' sent those who wanted to join him out to places where their presence might perhaps be important. He made his followers really 'strangers on earth': according to Psalm 119.19, this is what people of God need to be. Dominicans are deliberately people without a home, people who are always looking for a home, and still have to find their home. From its beginning, the Franciscan movement was orientated on standing apart from the world of trade and money which was beginning to come into being in the twelfth century. Separated from the world as it was, people simply wanted to live in the house of Lady Poverty and mutual brotherhood. The emphasis is rather different in the Dominican attempt to follow the apostles in their task of going around without possessions or purses. The Dominican ideal is not so much a choice of becoming and remaining an outsider in principle. Dominicans are not concerned to be at home somewhere other than in this world, they are concerned with seeking to live in this world as strangers and to exist on what comes their way.

A stranger is someone who constantly discovers that he has no home to live in and who therefore can only look for one. Such strangers see the situation in which they find themselves with fresh eyes. They perceive abuses more keenly than those with a fixed home, because they experience them personally. But they also see more clearly the good things that are on offer because they are dependent on them. A house is by definition good for the person who lives in it: it offers protection from the weather, the wind and from dangers. To a stranger who has access only to an open, hospitable house it is clear that only such a house can be said to be truly 'good'.

In my view, accepting the invitation to allow oneself to be made a stranger is an important element of a Dominican spirituality. It can lead to people literally taking a nomadic initiative and going into strange areas where indeed they are not at home but must wait to see whether they find a good place to live in and whether their new land proves habitable for them. But it can also mean that people are not opposed to the ongoing changes to which their world and their existence are subject, and allow these changes constantly to show them how to look at the situation in a new way and to seek their place in it. I honestly think that this is the most important contribution of the Dominican tradition to a spirituality which is tailored to our time. Time and again, and apparently at an ever faster pace, people are driven out of situations in which they were at home. Government decisions and natural disasters make them flee; economic developments make them uncertain; social, cultural and religious changes involve them in a life-long search for security, a search for who they are at the deepest level, under all the adaptations and metamorphoses that they need to make. The Dominican tradition offers footholds for surviving in the midst of these new developments. Survival comes not by finding a place outside them to live in, but by becoming completely part of them without being overwhelmed by them.

For in Dominican history the flood of contemporary developments has sometimes led to the discovery of new, surprising traces of God in unexpected places. This is already true of the origin of the Dominican movement, at a time when the cities were growing quickly and the whole of society was undergoing a decisive change. What for a long time had seemed an eternal order proved capable of change through human reason and human effort. For example, it turned out to be possible to get a greater harvest from the earth by organizing agriculture differently and one could acquire hitherto unattainable wealth by engaging in trade skilfully. No longer were people's fates determined by the situation into which they were born. Because money became increasingly important, it proved possible to gain a better social position through good luck and one's own effort. In short, the mobility which is characteristic of the Dominican life from the beginning is doubtless connected with the mobility which was becoming evident in the society of the twelfth and thirteenth centuries. It urgently confronts people with the question: what now is essential to life in the spiritual sense?

A new world

But in this chapter we shall dwell on another example of how social and cultural changes lead Dominicans to make important religious discoveries. The fifteenth century was dynamic in a hitherto unprecedented way. A 'new world' literally opened up. This dynamic dragged Dominican people along with it and led them on new ways, quite literally, but also spiritually and theologically.

When in 1492 Christopher Columbus discovered for Europe the continent that was later to be called America, it emerged that people lived there who had never come into contact with Christianity. At this time the Dominicans were firmly bound by all kinds of monastic rules and customs, like extended choral prayer and strictly regulated fasting. Such a life is possible only for those who feel at home in an ordered, well-organized environment. So the Dominicans did not react immediately to the discovery of the New World. Perhaps in the course of time they remembered Dominic, who had always felt that the conclusion of the Gospel of Matthew, 'Go and make disciples of all nations' (28.19), spoke very strongly to him. All his life he had wanted to go and preach the gospel to the Cumani, the people who lived in the north of Europe, on the edge of the then civilized world. However, it is more probable that the Dominicans were afraid of losing too much ground to other religious orders, especially the Franciscans. Be this as it may, in 1508 the then Master General of the Dominican Order, Tómas de Vio – in theological circles better known as Cajetan – decided to start a mission project in what was then called the West Indies. In February 1509 the first Dominicans travelled out from Spain and in 1510 the first Dominican monastery was built in Santo Domingo, in the present-day Dominican Republic. In this way

Dominican history came to be directly woven into the dynamic of conquest and colonization which to a large degree governed developments in Europe and had great consequences for the rest of the world.

However, Dominican history is dynamic not just by virtue of this dynamic, but also *vis-à-vis* this dynamic. Directly after Columbus' first landing the pope gave the Spanish king the right to preach the Christian faith in America. When Columbus travelled to the New World for the second time in 1493, he had a number of religious on board to fulfil this aim. They were given the commission by the king of Spain 'to take all possible pains to lead the inhabitants ... towards conversion to our holy faith'. Thus an attempt was made to give the Spanish actions in America the appearance of mission, of disseminating the message of the gospel. What in fact happened, though, was a violent conquest of new territories and an exploitation of the indigenous population. So exceptionally abhorrent was this exploitation that they perished in great numbers of exhaustion or hunger, or killed themselves and their children out of sheer despair. However, from the beginning there were also missionaries who saw that the conquests had far more to do with greed than with an urge to preach the Christian faith. Among them the Dominicans played a prominent role.

The Dominican Bartolomé de Las Casas (1484-1566) passionately attacked the crimes and abuses, which he called *The Destruction of the West Indies*. He was to earn the title 'protector of the Indians':

> To the present day the Spaniards have done nothing but tear the Indians to pieces, slaughtering them, tormenting them, outraging them, torturing them and seeking to kill them, with cruelties as novel as they are unprecedented. These surpass all that anyone has previously seen, heard of or read about ... So they have brought it about that of the three million natives which I saw with my own eyes inhabiting the island of Hispaniola [where Columbus landed], there are now only two hundred left.

In his later works Las Casas described in the most gruesome details the events which he only hints at here. His reports are of the utmost importance for a good picture of Dominican spirituality. His writings do not just depict a history which otherwise would have disappeared along with its victims, nor do they just bear witness to a moral indignation which is still impressive. These descriptions and this witness are at the same time a way of dealing with the Christian tradition which in principle is dynamic. According to Las Casas, Christian faith is not limited to church tradition but can come to light only in confrontation with reality as it is, in his case with the new reality of the colonization of America and its consequences.

The mobility of history upsets fixed thought patterns. For those who allow themselves to be taught through this experience with the attentiveness of a stranger, literally unknown traces of God then come to light.

'A voice crying in the wilderness'

Las Casas wrote his book *The Destruction of the West Indies* in 1542. However, to see the spiritual significance of this book and his later writings we need to go further back in time.

The Uruguayan writer Eduardo Galeano, in his kaleidoscopic history of Latin America entitled *Memory of Fire*, calls the appearance of the Dominican Antonio de Montesinos on the Fourth Sunday of Advent in 1511 'the first protest'. By that he means the first protest against the Spanish conquest and domination, the first protest against the torture and murder of the Indians. In fact it seems that the small community of Santo Domingo, of which de Montesinos formed a part, was the first really to pay attention to the fate of the indigenous population.

Because the Spanish conquest of the American continent was presented as a Christianization, the colonists were officially obliged to give the inhabitants of the region the religious instruction that they were due. But, as Galeano writes with much empathy, the colonists – 'the farmers from Extremadura and the shepherds from Andalusia', the 'adventurers bought with fine promises on the steps of the cathedral in Seville', the 'flea-ridden captains' and 'the condemned who had to choose between America and prison or the gallows' – had something else in mind. They were in search of the 'golden mountains and the naked princesses' that they had been told about. For their part, the Dominicans saw the preaching of the gospel as their special responsibility. In 1510, through Pedro de Córdoba, they urged the colonists that if these could not fulfil this task themselves, the Indians were to be sent to them. Although their preaching found a hearing and according to witnesses was in any case listened to attentively by the Indians, the Dominicans of Santo

Domingo began increasingly to feel strangers in life as it was organized in the New World. They began to model themselves on John the Baptist, of whom the gospel says that he was a voice crying in the wilderness: 'Prepare the way of the Lord, make his paths straight' (Luke 3.4).

The fact that it did not prove easy to bring the Indians to Christianity convinced many Spaniards that their hearts were a wilderness in which the voice of preaching sounded in vain. According to the current opinion their stubbornness showed that they fully deserved their harsh treatment by the Spanish colonists. It was therefore a real revolution when de Montesinos and his followers did not seem to regard the hearts of the Indians as the wilderness in which their voice called in vain. They proclaimed the bewildering message that the true wilderness consisted in the situation, in which both the Indians and the preaching of the gospel had to suffer, and that these two things were connected. The Dominicans of the community of Santo Domingo felt less and less that they could begin from current views about the preaching of the gospel, and less and less took as the starting point of their life and thought the rules which had been laid down by the Spanish king – who in his turn had been given the right to do this by the pope.

This ultimately resulted in them raising the hitherto unheard-of question whether what was being proclaimed in the New World in word and deed was really the gospel of salvation and liberation. The Christianity that the conquerors brought had certainly been authorized by the king and the pope. But did it also have a good and wholesome effect? Did it bear witness to the *Deus salutaris,* the God of salvation who is at its centre – or who the Dominicans were convinced needed to be at its centre? For them, gradually the most important criterion in judging the situation came to be not approval by king or pope, but the answer to the question of salvation.

A message that belongs to no one

Much later – according to oral tradition, he himself was not present – Bartolomé de Las Casas described how the whole community of Santo Domingo studied and reflected. The members of the community set life as it was imposed on the Indians alongside the principles of law and justice. And finally their feeling was that they had to conclude that the Spanish colonial system was the wilderness in which the voice of the God of justice and righteousness was resounding in vain.

The events which followed have been described often, and indeed they are extremely dramatic. The Dominicans invited the colonists into their church, telling them that something important was going to be said. Antonio de Montesinos was put forward by his fellow brethren as their best preacher. And de Montesinos spoke with great aplomb about the truth which his fellow brethren and himself had discovered together.

> To ensure that you understand it, I, who represent the voice of Christ in the wilderness of this island, have gone into this pulpit. Therefore you must listen attentively, not just with half an ear, but with all your senses. This voice is so new to you that you have never heard it before, and it is so forbidding, harsh, clear and dangerous that you never thought you would hear it.

What is special about this address does not lie in the rhetoric, which for many people today would indicate too great a certainty that the preacher was speaking the 'Word of God'. Rather, what is special is that the Dominicans of Santo Domingo evidently thought – and that must indeed have been unprecedentedly new for their audience – that in this situation the Word of God was not to be found first of all in the sacraments, nor was it guarded by those who held office in the church. It was not even to be heard first of all in the biblical writings or in the Catholic tradition. The Dominicans of Santo Domingo proclaimed that the word of God rang out above all among the Indians, in their suffering and their fate, in their patient protest about what was being done to them, a protest which was invisible to most of the colonists.

For Antonio de Montesinos and his fellow Dominicans the message of the gospel evidently belonged to no one. It was proclaimed to everyone, including Christians, from outside in a way which no one could predict beforehand. Surprisingly enough, in 'the wilderness of this island' God's voice rang out from the abhorrent situation in which the Indians found themselves. It proved impossible for the Christian tradition to function as a divinely-willed home in which one could dwell in protected calm. On the contrary, it made those who took it seriously hear once again an unprecedented divine voice which made them strangers in their situation, but which in this way called for improvement in the midst of the situation.

Everything depends on the perspective. It is possible to see the opposition of the Indians to their Christianization as a sign that they are putting themselves in the position of the heathen people over against Israel. If this is the case, according to the stories in the Bible, short shrift may be made of them. But for de Montesinos and his followers this opposition is a quiet voice which calls in the wilderness of their suffering and is a stimulus to see their fate with attentiveness and compassion. As a result of this the Dominicans of Santo Domingo become strangers in the existing situation, and what is generally regarded as the foundation of thought and action becomes a question as large as life. By what right do the Spaniards keep the Indians in slavery? By what right do they give them so little to eat that they die of hunger, neglect to see that their diseases are treated, and take no trouble to give them any instruction? De Montesinos ended his historic sermon on the First Sunday of Advent 1511 with the following crucial sentences, which were rightly to become famous.

> Are they not human beings? Do they not have rational souls? Are you not then obliged to love them as you love yourselves? Do you not understand that? Do you not grasp that? How is it that you sleep so soundly, so lethargically?

But however impressive these words may sound now, at the time when they were spoken de Montesinos remained a voice calling in the wilderness.

Dwelling in the voice that calls

De Montesinos' sermon above all provoked indignation among his audience. The colonial authorities complained to the Dominicans that they were preaching something completely new, but they had already said that themselves. When the Spanish king heard of the events, he once again confirmed 'the right of the crown and the solid theological and canonical foundation of the service that the Indians perform for Christians'. He did not go into the question whether it was just that the Christians should keep the Indians in slavery. He responded that it was legitimate in accordance with existing law and recalled 'the favour and gift which our Holy Father Pope Alexander VI has bestowed on us of all these islands and lands'.

Here there is every appearance that de Montesinos' sermon did not cause God's voice to be heard where the community of Santo Domingo had heard it, in the fate of the Indians.

Even Bartolomé de Las Casas, who in 1511 was still the owner of gold mines, land and Indians, who had grown rich in the New World and was perhaps among those who heard de Montesinos' sermon, was only truly to be converted to his view three years later. For Las Casas, reading a text from the Wisdom of Jesus Sirach was decisive:

> The sacrifice of an offering unjustly acquired is a mockery ... The Most High takes no pleasure in offerings from the godless, multiplying sacrifices will not give pardon for sin. Offering sacrifice from the property of the poor is as bad as slaughtering a son before his father's eyes (Sirach 34.21-24).

Las Casas sees the religious situation of the New World depicted here: God's children are being killed, and that is thought to be a service to the God in whose image and likeness they were after all created. He parted with his possessions, entered the Dominican Order and became an indefatigable accuser of the Spanish conquerors and the chronicler of the suffering of the Indians. He too now felt that the voice of God rang out in their suffering. And as that was a voice which resounded in the wilderness, he was prepared to remain in that same wilderness, if need be for the rest of his life.

Although Las Casas' writings and activities were ultimately to make him famous, during his lifetime he was above all a controversial figure, and was to remain so. Las Casas is the symbol of the new piety which the Dominicans discovered in the New World: dedication to the unheard-of, attention to the holy that protests against its infringement in a voice which cries in the wilderness. He is *par excellence* the model of someone who allows this voice to make him a stranger in his own situation, someone who only wants to live where this voice is heard. The Chilean poet Pablo Neruda speaks about Las Casas' dedication to the fate of the Indians as 'the eternity of tenderness above the flood of chastizing' which is their history. Neruda invokes Las Casas in times of fear and discouragement:

> Come today to my house, Padre, come in with me,
> I shall show you the letters, the misery
> of my people, who are persecuted.

I shall show you the old suffering.

The piety which in the eyes of this Communist poet had previously been as 'vain as an abandoned cathedral' is in his view transformed in Las Casas into 'active resistance', into respect for the resistance and opposition which are already there, in active dedication to the cry which resounds in the midst of suffering.

But there is something to be said against the picture that Neruda paints of Las Casas. He models Las Casas' fight against the injustice that was done to the Indians too much on the appearance of later revolutionaries. When he speaks of believing as an 'armed heart' for which reason is the 'titanic material', he wrongly makes Las Casas a kind of proto-Communist, almost a Lenin *avant la lettre*. But in contrast to most nineteenth- and twentieth-century revolutionaries, neither Antonio de Montesinos nor Bartolomé de Las Casas are concerned with 'making' salvation happen. They direct their attention to the places where this salvation announces itself to their perception in faith, where it proves to live in the longing or comes to light in the protest. De Montesinos and Las Casas live out faith as a form of dedication, as trust in the voice which cries in the wilderness, convinced that this voice will ultimately prove a good and safe place to live.

A thinking heart

Here in fact a new connection between believing and thinking arises, as Neruda suggests in his poem about Las Casas. If believing is no longer seen as accepting the religious tradition but as dedication to what offers itself in living reality as traces of God, then it automatically ends up as thinking in the direction in which these traces point. As we saw, Neruda speaks about Las Casas' spirituality in terms of an 'armed heart', a being touched that ends up in struggle. However, it seems more adequate to use an expression which comes from the Jewish writer Etty Hillesum, murdered in Auschwitz in 1943: 'the thinking heart'. For time and again Las Casas' thought is driven by respect for the sufferer; it is a thought that because of this respect cannot do other than protest against the suffering and try to fathom out existing reality in the light of it. It does so to make it possible to see where a wholesome change is announcing itself and where it is possible to play on it. In the sixteenth century the dedicated attentiveness to the fate of the Indians and reflection on its consequences did not just lead to a new look at history, as in the case of Las Casas, but also to important new theoretical insights. The Dominican moral theologian Francisco de Vitoria (1483-1546), who was already famous in his own time, never went to America. However, the stories of what was going on there led him radically to rethink the basis of the relationship between peoples. He writes:

> If we then perceive that so many people have been killed and so many innocents have been robbed and attacked in their possessions, and that so many landowners have been robbed of their property, we can doubt whether that has been done rightly and whether no injustice has been perpetrated.

The insight that the action of the Spaniards did not back up their own claim to stand in the service of God's salvation also makes de Vitoria a stranger. He, the jurist, becomes a stranger in the legal system of his land. The discussion about the reasons cited to defend the Spanish activity in America leads him to ask the fundamental question how peoples really relate to one another and how they need to deal with one another. In his view, the fact that people make contact with one another emerges from the human – 'natural' – tendency *par excellence* to achieve friendship and a bond with others. In his view, the fact that this tendency is peculiar to human beings means on the one hand that no single people may cut themselves off from contact with other peoples. And on the other hand, any people is allowed to claim that other peoples should respect its right to look for the good life, free from any constraints.

Developing these basic notions in more detail, de Vitoria lays the foundation for later international law. But in the framework of the present book, what is certainly just as important is that the way in which his faith was affected by the fate of the Indians led him on untrodden paths. The mobility which since the time of Dominic has characterized the world in which we live ensures that constantly new questions emerge. New choices have to be made from a believing and spiritual perspective, too, and therefore new situations call to be lived through in a religious way and new questions call to be thought through theologically. The insight that old answers and old concepts are not enough is part of being a stranger that is fundamental to a Dominican spirituality. This is equally true of the insight that one can occupy this stranger's position. Time and again new words and concepts will offer themselves. The quest of God arises in the quest for new and wholesome ways that can be taken. In pondering, making and responding to the choices with which present-day men and women are faced, we discover new facets of the God of salvation. According to the basic Dominican conviction we have to live by these revelations: material, spiritual and intellectual.

This brings us back to the core around which the texts in this book constantly circle. The tradition of the religious life as a whole and the Dominican tradition in particular consists of a long series of attempts to stand in the space of God's presence and to understand oneself within it. Time and again, the explorations that have been undertaken here make it clear that in the Dominican tradition this means sharing in the contemporary longing for salvation, seeing traces of God in the salvation that lights up, and dedicating oneself to these traces and trusting them

A shared eye and ear

This has consequences for the way in which we relate to one another. The rules which the Dominican movement devised in the course of time for forming, organizing and maintaining Dominican communities try to formulate these consequences. They are not always successful here, but the starting points that they use are important. In all the Dominican rules 'the Dominican mission' is central: bringing to light in word and deed what is holy and wholesome. But the starting point of the regulations of the Dominican religious life is that this mission is not just a 'task', a work, that need only be carried out. All the regulations for Dominican communities and associations are based on the assumption that seeking what is holy, being dedicated to it and carrying it out are not just important in an objective sense but form a good basis for giving a wholesome form to one's own existence. Furthermore, the starting point is that people who want to orientate themselves on the Dominican tradition also in fact come upon traces of the holy in their own lives. They discover ways of dedicating themselves to it; they find forms of living by trust in the Holy One who reveals himself in it, and succeed in communicating what occupies them here. In other words, the presupposition of all

Dominican associations is that people are always already occupied in discovering the religious life in the Dominican sense, in the places where they live and the situations in which they live.

If that is to be done well, the support and correction of others is indispensable. Therefore the Dominican life is orientated on others: this is in order to strengthen one another in dedication, to connect experiences together, to exchange the forms that have been discovered, to speak and try out what is perceived as a trace of the God of salvation. Just as the church, according to a well-known slogan, needs to be in a state of constant reform – *ecclesia semper reformanda* – so the Dominican movement also needs constantly to be refounded. Loyalty to the Dominican tradition takes shape in an ongoing consultation of everyone with everyone else about what authentic Dominican life is in the given circumstances.

With a view to this ongoing re-founding, from the beginning of the Order the Dominican regime has been strongly democratic. Leaders have been chosen by all concerned for a limited period. At every level of organization, councils operate which have the function of representing the different views among Dominicans and to set them against each other. The importance of this democratic form of government was emphasized in the text which was officially added to the regulations for the life of the Dominican brothers at the end of the 1960s. It is said that this ensures

> that the mission of the Order is furthered and that the Order itself is renewed in an appropriate way. This ongoing evaluation is . . . necessary . . . for the sake of the Order's own calling, which compels it to a presence in the world that is appropriate to every generation.

It has been suggested that the democratic structure of the government of religious orders, especially also of the Dominicans, influenced the rise of the democratic state after the French Revolution. Be this as it may, it is important to see that Dominican democracy has a different orientation from that of the present-day liberal state. As a liberal form of the state, democracy has the aim of exerting regulated influence on the way in which rule is exercised. The basic idea is that of the sovereignty of the people: the government must express and carry out the will of the people. The aim of democracy as a form of Dominican religious life is not first and foremost to give all those concerned the right to speak. They have the right and even the duty to speak, but they do so with a view to the aim of the Dominican movement as a whole. It is the function of Dominican democracy to rediscover and reformulate the Dominican mission together.

The Dominican mission takes form in what Dominicans do and say in all the places where they live and work. Therefore it is only by consulting together that they can discover how this mission can be formulated better, encouraged more strongly and supported more effectively. Dominicans are convinced that insight arises into the religious situation in which we live when people with different backgrounds and skills come together and compare their views. For example, one person may know about community work in inner-city areas, another may have a good knowledge of the media or art, a third may be involved in building up a local faith community, a fourth may be at home in specialist theological discussions and a fifth and a sixth may have a career in professional life or government, or be heart and soul a parent or a grandparent, and through a long stay in the 'cell of self-knowledge' have attained insight into what in religious terms it means to live in present-day society and culture. In other words, to form a Dominican association means to form a common eye and ear: looking for traces of the Holy One, focused on the voices which resound in the wilderness that our society so often is, and concerned to dedicate oneself to these traces and to give a hearing to these voices.

Dominican community

I am convinced that Dominican spirituality is not only important for people who form part of a Dominican association, but also for all those who are concerned to live a religious life in the midst of the possibilities and problems raised by contemporary existence. So Dominican democracy is important not only for people within the Dominican movement but also for anyone who with others wants to dwell in the sphere of the divine Presence. The way of democracy is not the short way and often also is the goal: the formation of a community in which the mutual differences do not lead to strife but to a fuller view of what is happening, a view of how the Holy is present in the midst of it, though this is realized only very partially.

Only a community which is democratic in the Dominican sense of the word will ultimately be a place of rest in the midst of mobility and turbulence. It is not a matter of shutting ourselves off from the unrest but of being a space of common attentiveness to what is happening, what holiness can be seen within it, and what of the divine rings out. Along this way, in the midst of all kinds of division and fragmentation, a new form of unanimity can arise. The Rule of Augustine says:

> The chief motivation for your sharing life together is to live harmoniously in the house and to have one heart and one soul seeking God (cf. Acts 4.32).

First of all. What is first of all at the same time proves to be what is last of all. As is often the case.

Postscript: Dominican: An identity that is not an identity

Timothy Radcliffe, the English Dominican who since 1992 has been Master of the Dominican Order, has written a remarkable article about identity and religious life. In it he first sets out why in a society like ours, full of movement and uncertainty, it is so important for people to have an identity of their own. When everything around us is changing and proves to be unreliable at crucial moments, when the economy can suddenly make us unemployed or we can unexpectedly take on new responsibilities, when relationships keep breaking down and we constantly make new discoveries; when we constantly have to play yet other roles, the question of who we are in our authentic selves must quickly arise. Timothy Radcliffe then goes on to point out that in a period in which identity becomes increasingly important, members of religious orders within the Catholic Church seem to have lost their specific identity. Since the 1960s groups of people have felt an increasing need to distinguish themselves from one another by clothing or hairstyle. But at the beginning of the 1960s the religious orders increasingly began to set aside their distinctive garb.

The striking thing is that Timothy Radcliffe does not argue for a restoration of the specific and visible identity of members of religious orders. Certainly, he pleads for older religious to understand the younger ones, who sometimes seem to find support in the traditional symbols of religious identity. But the main thrust of his argument is that true religious life means standing apart from the recognizable signs of a unique identity. Where many people derive their identity in our culture from their sexuality and their capacity to score sexually, members of religious orders, as Radcliffe points out, reject a sexual relationship. Where for many people the house that they live in, the car that they drive or the designer clothing that they buy determine who they are, members of religious orders opt for a life in poverty. And where in our society making one's own choice of how to live, what to buy, where to have a home and what to do, by one's self and free from compulsion, is the image of the complete and adult person, members of religious orders dedicate themselves to obedience to a voice which comes from elsewhere.

I was struck by Timothy Radcliffe's article. In his remark that religious life meant not having one's own fixed identity, I recognized what I thought I understood about Dominican spirituality. Religious life consists in openness to the identity which you have been given and which you discover, not detached from the circumstances in which you find yourself more or less by chance, as a consequence of deliberate decisions or through the whims of fate, but at the heart of them. At the same time, though, in the end I think that Timothy Radcliffe does not go far enough. He does not seem to see how much his vision fundamentally relativizes the difference between religious in the strict sense, as laid down in canon law, and 'laity'. And if he does realize it, he doesn't seem to draw any conclusions from it.

This little book is in a sense an attempt to draw these conclusions. I have sought to present the Dominican tradition and the spirituality to which it bears witness as a support and a guide for people who are not so much 'religious' in a formal sense but want to lead their lives, with all the personal peculiarities and historical chances that go with them, in a religious way. I have tried to make clear what I have gradually become convinced of: that the Dominican tradition has always belonged above all to such people and that its future therefore also depends on them. Anyone who wants to continue the Dominican tradition must not want to continue the Dominican tradition as such. Together with others, he or she must investigate what a Dominican life can be, heart and soul, mind and body, hands and feet. What does it mean to be focused on traces of the God of salvation and liberation and to devote oneself completely to this God?

That Dominican life has constantly to be discovered and rediscovered has two important consequences. First of all it means that what Dominican religious life and Dominican spirituality are can never be found in a text or a document. Different readers of the earlier versions of this book complained that it was very difficult. Now I will not claim to be completely free of the tendency to make things more complicated than they need be, but I honestly think that in principle it is impossible just to explain what the characteristics and the specific properties of a Dominican spirituality are quite simply and clearly. To write about Dominican spirituality is to explore Dominican spirituality as one writes, until what is to be found begins to speak to one's own situation. Thus it is almost inevitable that a book on Dominican spirituality should have 'An Exploration' as a subtitle; one can write only about it while exploring it. The chapters of this book and the introduction are in fact essays which I hope can lure readers into sharing in the explorations that they make. In my view, what I have brought to light about Dominican spirituality in these pages applies to both writing and reading. These are forms of being open to what offers itself – always in a different way from what one thinks, a way which can never be compelled – as holy, as a trace of the Holy.

That Dominican spirituality must constantly be discovered and rediscovered means, secondly, that every text about it necessarily has a personal colouring. An attentive reader of earlier versions of the book pointed out that many thoughts occur in it that she knew were dear to me and that I had also expressed elsewhere. She asked whether this meant that I was so deeply Dominican, or whether I was reading back my favourite ideas into the Dominican tradition. I don't really have an answer to this question. After all that I have seen, heard and read in the meantime, I think that I can say that the view developed here is not directly a projection of personal ideas on to Dominican history. The reactions of other Dominicans to what I have written also make it clear that my view is not so peculiar that they cannot recognize themselves in it. At the same time I am fully aware, with a mixture of pride and confusion, that much of what I present here as Dominican spirituality has never been formulated in this way, in these terms or with this emphasis. I really believe that I have found something valuable and authentically Dominican and therefore I have been glad to present it to the reader. But whether the light that I think I can see and to which I call attention is really the light that reflects God's life is for me too an open question. I can only hope that there are readers who will also pose this question to themselves in all seriousness.

When in the Netherlands a group of people who had long been orientated on Dominican tradition refounded the Dominican Lay Community of the Netherlands on 24 October 1999, we chose a shawl as a symbol of our Dominican dedication. It does not cover our ordinary clothing, like a habit, but shows how we go through our daily and not so daily existence of work and leisure, of love, friendship and parenthood, with dedication and effort. Our bond as Dominicans is expressed above all in what we contribute and what we want to contribute, to the future of this movement. We do not want to fit into the Dominican tradition in the form in which it has come down to us. We want to explore this tradition – which has become a support and a signpost for us in our lives – more closely, starting from our own positions, not because we know better, but because we take it completely seriously. To do this we seek one another's company and that of others within the Dominican movement in the broadest sense of the word. For that reason we call upon one another's commitment, quality and skills and want our commitment, qualities and skills to be called upon. In our view, a Dominican movement which does this with people and a Dominican tradition which functions as support for it can gain an important significance and thus has a future. In the end, what this book seeks to do is to make a contribution to this meaning and this future.

Appendix: Dominican Spirituality

Edward Schillebeeckx

For the most part people live by stories. I myself live by my own story. When I became a Dominican I linked my life story with the family story of the Dominicans; as a result, my life story took on a new orientation and I picked up the thread of the story of the Order in my own way. So my own life has become part of the Dominican family story: a chapter in it. Through the story of the Order I have attained my own identity. Stories of the Dominican Order keep us together as Dominicans. Without stories we should lose our memories, fail to find our own place in the present and remain without hope or expectation for the future. Thus as Dominicans we form a group by virtue of being our own storytelling community, which hands down its own traditions within the wider story of the many religious communities, within the all-embracing story of the great community of the church, and within the even greater community of humankind. This makes us our own special family, recognizable from all kinds of family characteristics. Some are major, some are minor, but none of them can be hidden.

In saying this, I have already said something about Dominican spirituality. The story of my life can be my own life story only in so far as it has become a chapter of the Dominican family story. The story of my own life extends and enriches the history of Dominican spirituality, while as a small – almost infinitesimally small – chapter in it, it is at the same time relativized and criticized by the already older and wider story of the Dominican family. This makes me ask whether I really am not distorting this family story. So I am already sceptical about all those who would suggest 'one's own insight' or 'one's own experience' to others as a norm for Dominican spirituality. Furthermore, thank God, there are still Dominicans alive today. In other words, our story is not yet exhausted, completely told; there is still something to be said.

A first conclusion already follows from this: a definitive all-round definition of Dominican spirituality cannot be given. You cannot make a final judgment on a story which is still going strong. We can only trace some of the main lines in the plot of the story, which has now been handed down for seven centuries in constantly different ways: the one basic story has been told in countless other languages to constantly different listeners, and has varied depending on their cultural, historical circumstances and the nature of their church.

The basic story which stands at the beginning of our own Dominican storytelling community is of fundamental importance here. But the origin of any relevant story usually blurs into an obscure past which is difficult to reconstruct historically. Dominic (1170-1223), the origin of the Dominican family story, did not write any books. Nevertheless, through laborious historical reconstruction which extracts the 'real Dominic' from all kinds of legends (so typical of the Middle Ages), we have sufficient firm ground under our feet. In particular, though Dominic may not have left behind any books or documents, what he did leave behind as a living legacy was the Dominican movement, the Order, a group of people who wanted to carry on his work in his footsteps. The Dominican story therefore begins with Dominic and his first companions; together they stand at the beginning of what was to become the Dominican family story. They gave the story its theme: they set its tone.

However, this story, often retold and sometimes rewritten, is in itself a particular way in which the thread of an already older story, that of Jesus of Nazareth, is taken up and continued in a new manner. This already brings us to a second conclusion. Dominican spirituality is valid only in so far as it takes up the story of Jesus and brings it up to date in its own way. In its Decree on the Renewal of Religious Life, the Second Vatican Council said that 'to follow Jesus' is the ultimate and supreme norm of any form of religious life (*suprema regula*, no.2). Dominican spirituality is therefore subject to the criterion of the sources of all Christian life. This also means that even the Dominican spirituality of Dominic and his first followers is not directly an absolute law for Dominicans. A fuller and more sophisticated knowledge of the story of Jesus which has become possible since then (e.g. through new devotional experiences based on the Bible or through more refined exegesis of scripture) may therefore lead us to different emphases from those of Dominic and his followers. For according to the Council's Decree on Religious Renewal, this renewal must happen in the first place through a return 'to the sources of all Christian life' (no.2), the gospel of Jesus Christ (Mark 1.1). That source is never exhausted and always offers new possibilities, for which even Dominic himself did not know the all-embracing 'Open Sesame'.

At the same time this implies that the story of every religious Order must be judged as a part or, better, as a modulation of the greater story of the 'community of God', the church ('a participation in the life of the church': ibid., no. 2). Here the Council points to the 'present-day projects' of the church: biblical, liturgical, dogmatic, pastoral, ecumenical, missionary and social. That is, Dominican spirituality essentially presupposes a critical involvement in the very specific needs and problems of today's church in its historical circumstances; it cannot be an isolated cultivation of our own 'Dominican' garden alongside the ongoing life of the world and the church.

Given all this, however, governed by the gospel and subject to the constant historical criticism that it exercises, and at the same time as a concrete historical feature of the necessary major projects of the church in the world here and now, in fact 'the original inspiration of one's own religious institution' (thus the Council's Decree on Religious Life, no.2) is the basic theme of the Dominican family story, and is therefore normative. Here the Council Decree points not only to the original 'specific project' *(propria proposita)* of the founder, but also to the Order's 'own religious traditions', at least in so far as these are sound *(sanae traditiones)*; that is, to the 'spiritual heritage' of a religious order: its spirituality.

The third conclusion may therefore be that Dominican spirituality is valid as a special mode of the church's task 'to follow Jesus', especially – for us – in the footsteps and the inspiration of Dominic, as this inspiration has constantly provided new light and direction in the best moments of the history of the Order. Therefore we must clearly bring this basic historical story to mind, for in the course of time the Dominican community has also had a broken relationship to its own origins. When the Inquisition brought, for example, Joan of Arc to the stake, the Dominicans involved were essentially contradicting Dominic's inspiration and orientation. People had become deaf and blind to the origin of new charismata: this was an essentially un-Dominican attitude.

As a third criterion for renewed religious life, the same Decree of the Council gives the relationship of the story of Jesus and the original basic story (for us, of the Dominicans) to the altered circumstances of the time (no. 22). This implies that Dominican spirituality cannot be defined purely by a reference to the original story or purely by a reference to the further modulations and updating of this basic story in the course of the history of the Order, though this is presupposed. Dominican spirituality also involves the way in which we live out this Dominican family story here and now, in our time. Dominican spirituality does not indicate simply how things were 'at the beginning' or in the course of the history of the Order. In that case we would simply be writing a historical report of the way in which Dominicans were inspired in former times. But historical knowledge is not yet spirituality. Thus someone who was a good historian but not a Dominican could reconstruct it better than we could. If it is not to be purely the 'history' of a spirituality (and furthermore, if it is not to become an empty ideology), Dominican spirituality is a living reality today; it is handed on (or distorted) by Dominicans living now, who reshape the Dominican family story here and now with an eye to the situation in the world and the church, the cultural historical situation of the moment.

Thus the fourth conclusion runs as follows: without a living relationship to the present, any talk about Dominican spirituality remains a purely historical preoccupation with the past of the Order (often an excuse for neglecting tasks which are urgent now). Dominican spirituality is a living reality which is to be realized among us now. Otherwise we simply repeat stories which others have told for a long time, as though we ourselves did not have to write our own chapter in what is of course a story which had already begun before us. Whereas now we do have to write a new chapter that is still unpublished, if after us anyone else is going to think it worth taking up the thread of this Dominican story again. If in fact we can, may and will write that new living chapter, I am certain that many young people, men and women, will again be drawn to continue the Dominican tradition after us. For any meaningful story has a power of attraction; it is retold, and no one can stop its snowball effect. Whether that happens, however, depends on the tone in which we write our chapter in the great Dominican family story and the tension it contains. Will it be a dull, unread little paragraph? Or will it be an alien story which does not take up the thread of the family story that has already begun, and so allows the Dominican story to die out, perhaps for good? Or will it become an attractive episode, attractive perhaps only because all that the hearer notices is that we are zealously in search of the real thread of the story, which for the moment we have lost track of? That too can also be an important part of the already old Dominican family story.

A 'golden thread' runs through the Dominican family story, from Dominic down to the present day. As may become evident, this golden thread sometimes runs across the fabric of Christianity – a fact that we must not obscure when we are writing our share in the great history of the Order. Provided that this golden thread is woven into our life story, however different it may be in content, we have in fact realized Dominican spirituality. 'Spirituality' is not spirituality so long as it is only described, whether in an assertive or an authoritarian tone. It is spirituality to the degree that is realized in practice – as a completely new rendering of an old Dominican melody.

How does this older melody go, this constantly recurring theme, this basic story?

I would say that it is a cross-grained story! In the twelfth century and at the beginning of the thirteenth there were two burning issues: a need for renewal in the priestly life and a need for renewal in the monastic life. The Fourth Lateran Council in 1215 dealt with the two problems separately, without any relation between them, and without connecting the two. This Council was not without its influence on Dominic who, as an Augustinian canon of Osma, on a journey to the south of France had already gathered round him a group of fellow workers to provide for the pressing needs of priestly care in the diocese of Toulouse, which had severe pastoral problems. Dominic saw the signs of the times. In the twelfth century, religious movements had arisen: a great many lay people joined them. The basic tendency of these movements was to combine gospel poverty with preaching, but they often had an anti-clerical tone. All kinds of clerical abuses had prompted the question: does Christian preaching

require the permission of the church (the bishop), and invol
commissioning and sending by the church? Or is not religious life,
and life according to the gospel in the footsteps of the apostles (at
that time called the *vita apostolica*), itself a qualification for Christian
preaching? This last view was the standpoint of many religious
movements, whereas it was officially regarded as 'heresy' by the
Councils. We could say that the heretical movements of that time
were inspired by the gospel and Christ, while the official preachers,
though orthodox, did not lead a life in accordance with the gospel –
at least to all outward appearances – and were completely embedded
in feudal structures. All manifestations of this new religious
movement – above all in France, Italy, Germany and the
Netherlands (the rich countries of that time) – show striking
common features (independently of each other): living out the
gospel *sine glossa* (without compromises). Its spirituality was
characterized by a deep devotion to the humanity of Jesus:
following the poor Jesus. (This happened under the influence of
the Cistercian movement and the Gregorian reform.)

At the same time there was clear influence from the
contemplative, Greek Byzantine East (through the Crusaders and
cloth merchants). The situation became more serious when these
gospel movements came into contact with dualistic Eastern
movements which arrived in the West through the Slavonic lands
of the Danube; they were called Cathars, a collective term for
Gnostic and dualistic trends. As a result the whole of the 'gospel
movement' became even more suspect to the church. The problem
became that of saving the gospel movement for the church and
mobilizing it against heresy. We must set the phenomenon of
Dominic against this historical background of all kinds of
enthusiastic revivals of evangelism, but on the periphery of the
official church. Dominic was not alone in seeing the problems in the
situation: Pope Innocent III, Bishop Diego, with whom Dominic
travelled to the south, and Francis of Assisi also saw it. With
outspoken realism, Dominic formulated a clear rescue programme.
He saw that an enormous potential for the gospel was being lost to
the church. Though trained in the already traditional canonical
priestly life, he was nevertheless sympathetic to these new counter-
experiments. But he saw quite clearly why they either kept failing
(splitting off into 'heretical' sects), or came to be incorporated once
again into traditional monastic life (e.g. the Premonstratensians). He

wanted to make these counter-movements authentic alternative forms of the church's evangelism, a church movement: he wanted as it were to 'live like the heretics' but 'teach like the church'.

Evangelism must be a challenge within the church; in other words it must be the church and not a sect. Dominic's own vision came near to this in that he saw the solution of the problems of the time in the combination – in one institution – of apostolic preaching (that is, preaching with a critical remembrance of the need for a proclamation endorsed by the pope or by the episcopate), and the *vita apostolica* (that is, radical evangelism: following Jesus like the apostles). He brought together organically, in one programme, the themes treated separately by the Fourth Lateran Council. Because this same Council, to some extent contrary to the personal views of Pope Innocent III, had forbidden all new forms of religious life and 'banned' unauthorized preaching, Dominic combined the best of traditional monastic life with the basic trends of the new counter-movements which had arisen all over Europe and which, to make the Christian proclamation credible, required a life commensurate with the gospel from those who proclaimed it. In so doing he broke down the feudal structures of the old monastic life: thus there arose a new form of religious life, the Order of Preachers, the Dominicans. Hence our earliest constitutions are largely made up of elements from the constitutions of traditional religious life, especially from the Norbertines and Cistercians (at that time the most lively religious institutions). However, Dominic and his first followers transformed these elements by the very purpose of the Order: apostolic itinerant preaching; that is, the new spirit of what were then modern, experimental gospel movements brought into the perspective of the church.

Dominic had been caught up in this spirit through his contact in the south of France with all this heretical gospel enthusiasm, which was shared by a broad spectrum of people, high and low. Through the structure of his Order, Dominic had weakened the economic stability which had been the basic principle of the older monastic institutions. On the basis of a *religious* criticism Dominic thus attacked the foundations of the feudal system (in church and society). Furthermore, the association of the contemplative monastic element with itinerant preaching resulted in a basic difference from the traditional form of monastic life. The new 'corporative' idea (a particular form of organization, as in the official guilds) was adapted to the religious institution: there was no 'monarchical' authority from above but a democratic form of government with a range of choices (democratic and personal). Paradoxically, Dominic's evangelism led to a new incarnation in secular structures, especially those of the rising democratic mediaeval bourgeoisie.

By thread and cross-thread, Dominic wove a new fabric, created a new religious programme. Thus the Dominican Order was born from the charisma of the combination of admonitory and critical recollection of the spiritual heritage of the old monastic and canonical religious life with the 'modernistic' religious experiment of the thirteenth century. Dominic had a fine sensitivity both to religious values from the past and to the religious promise for the future emanating from the modern experiments of his time. The Dominican Order was born out of this two-fold charisma. I would say that this is our *gratia originalis,* the grace at the origin of our Order.

Dominican spirituality is therefore in the first instance to be defined as a spirituality which, on the basis of admonitory and critical reflection on the heritage left behind by the past religious tradition, takes up critically and positively the cross-thread provided by whatever new religious possibilities for the future keep emerging among us. Therefore it can never be a *material* repetition of what our Dominican forebears have themselves done admirably. Nor, however, can it be an *uncritical* acceptance of whatever 'new movements' (in the mystical or political sense) are now evident in our midst. For Dominic, the essential thing was the question of truth. In his heart Dominic was ultimately one hundred per cent behind the new apostolic experiments of *preaching* combined with poverty, but – remembering the good achievements of the previous patterns of religious life – he unconditionally observed the guidelines laid down by the Fourth Lateran Council (1215) for any renewal of both priestly and religious life. His charisma was organically to combine two divergent guidelines and thus personally to extend the aims of this Council.

On the basis of this spirituality, which found expression in our very first Dominican Constitutions, the further history of the spirituality becomes understandable. This brings the historical, changing, cross-grained, new element into the very heart of Dominican spirituality. For example, the Constitutions from the years 1221-31 said: 'Our brothers may not study the books of pagan

writers (referring above all to Aristotle) and philosophers (what is
meant is Arabic philosophy, the great modernism in the Middle
Ages); far less may they study the secular sciences.' However, only
about twenty years later, Albert the Great and Thomas Aquinas
were to regard the study of secular sciences and the 'pagan
philosophers' as a necessary condition of the preparation and
formation of an appropriate Dominican apostolate. Thus on the
basis of an authentic Dominican spirituality these two Dominican
saints boldly went against a Dominican constitution set up in earlier
times and were therefore in opposition to what was then in fact
called official 'Dominican spirituality'. They did this – inspired by
what Dominic did in his time – so successfully that the definition
was later removed from the Constitutions by a General Chapter;
indeed, later Constitutions urged Thomas as a model (Raymond of
Penafort had centres for the study of Arabic built in Nursia and
Tunis). That is an authentically Dominican development, after the
heart of St Dominic, who himself tried to reconcile 'the past' and
new 'possibilities for the future'. (This brought with it the new
danger that Thomas would later cease to be a beacon pointing
towards the future and would become a closed frontier.) If no cross-
thread can be seen in the story that the Dominican perceives and
takes up again himself, there is every chance that Dominican
spirituality will fade; worse still, that on the basis of an 'established'
Dominican spirituality – which is a contradiction in terms – we shall
wrongly write off as apocryphal talk new attempts at a truly
Dominican spirituality. The greatest moments in the history of our
Order are when at the same time this history becomes anti-history
or a cross-thread: Dominic himself, Albert and Thomas, Savonarola,
Eckhardt, de Las Casas, Lacordaire, Lagrange, Chenu, Congar, to
name a few. However, at the same time Dominicans have
sometimes (in the first instance at least) run into difficulties with
the already established Dominican story when in an un-Dominican
way it has refused to take up the new cross-thread. Without
mistaking the fundamental worth, by which we are all supported, of
the many anonymous Dominicans who have quietly lived a
successful Dominican religious life (though their tranquillity can
have a broad influence and produce cross-grained stories within the
Order), nevertheless it only becomes clear what is typically
Dominican when Dominicans sometimes, following the example
of Dominic, reshape 'the old' and combine it with the dynamism of

constantly new and different forms. If this does not happen at regular intervals, then there is every chance that the well-known Dominican concern for truth will be dishonoured in an Inquisition and the new 'Dominican possibilities' are rejected. These possibilities may then come to life outside the Dominican family. I would not want to include this less rosy story – which is also part of our Order – in the golden thread of our family story, which is always in a state of constantly taking up the cross-thread again. However, the cross-thread sometimes ensures the continuity! The history of this cross-thread is the golden thread of the Dominican family story, woven into a broader, as it were more serene, whole. That St Ignatius of Loyola was shut up in the cellars of one of our monasteries because he shocked the people of his time with a new charisma is one of the many stories in which 'Dominican spirituality' has perversely become its opposite; it now shows us to be guilty of un-Dominican chauvinism. In other words, this is typical of times in which the Dominicans were no longer 'Dominican' and on the basis of their own 'established' position had already dubbed the new counter-thread heretical. The constantly new forms which Dominican spirituality must take in accordance with Dominic's basic story will emerge even more clearly, precisely through the moments in which we have failed in the past.

It is essential for Dominican spirituality to attend to God as God has already revealed himself to us in the past and to attend to the present-day 'signs of the time' in which the same God, who is faithful to us, makes his appeal. Any one-sidedness – in one-track, uncritical judgment either of the past or of what prove to be symptoms of the future in the present – is un-Dominican. Dominic submits the present, with its own possibilities of experiment, to comparison with the dangerous recollection of certain events and legacies from the past, just as at the same time he opens up the global past and gives it the stamp of the cross-grained experimental present: it is out of this kind of attitude that the Order was born. This must remain its 'genius'. The *présence à Dieu* and the *présence au monde* (as Lacordaire puts it) describe the very nature of Dominican spirituality throughout the history of the Order. And perhaps today we are going to see clearly that – in recollection of the religious past – the *présence au monde* or critical solidarity with the human world is the only possible mode of our *présence à Dieu*. At the same time this insight confirms the need for a critical recollection of the religious past in which the same *présence à Dieu* is always revealed in the communication of what were then the contemporary signs of the time. The 'modernism' of the Dominican Order lives on dangerous memories from the past. After what was almost a centuries-long sleep, Père Lacordaire and Master General Jandel were the ones who in the nineteenth century recalled the Dominican Order to its original charisma and brought about a break with the serene traditionalism to which the 'established order' had succumbed. 'Lacordaire' (and everything connected with that within our Dominican history) was in fact the rediscovery of the Order by itself. For the Lacordaire movement was nourished by the original charisma of the Order and as a result again raised the problem of 'Dominican spirituality'.

Some characteristics of Dominican spirituality are clear from this:

1. Belief in the absolute priority of God's grace in any human action: the theological direction of the Dominican life and its programme in relation to ethics, the world, society and the betterment of people. There must be no obsessive concern with the self but trust in God: I can trust God more than myself. The result is a tranquil and happy spirituality. God still gives an unexpected future to the limited meaning and scope of my own actions.

2. Religious life in the light of the gospel *(vita apostolica)* as the atmosphere in which the Dominican is *apostolic (salus animarum,* salvation as the aim of the activity of the Order): through preaching in all its forms. The result of that is *contemplari* and *contemplate aliis fradere* (i.e. the agreement between what a person proclaims and his own life; here Thomas Aquinas is contrasting the character of the mendicants with that of other religious institutions and at the same time connecting this with 'poverty': being free from financial worries). This general mendicant view became typically Dominican through the insertion of study as an essential element into the structure of this Dominican evangelism. This particular element was not characteristic of the mediaeval evangelical movements. 'Study is not the aim of the Order but an essential instrument for this work' (says Humbert of Romans in his commentary on the Constitutions). The failure of many gospel movements was also caused by a lack of thought. Furthermore, while the universities, which were only established at that time, had intensified the element of academic

study, at the same time they had concentrated it and centralized it so that there were no intellectuals in the dioceses. Dominic saw this, and therefore he incorporated study as an institutional element in the very organization of his Order. He would not have any monastery founded 'without a doctor in theology', and every monastery had to be a 'school of theology': a Dominican monastery is 'permanent instruction'. The distinction between study monasteries and pastoral monasteries is un-Dominican; both must be monasteries for study and pastoral ministry. Thomas Aquinas defended a religious institution 'founded for study'.

3. The 'Jesus spirituality' of the order – the 'humanity of Jesus' (Albert, Thomas, Eckhardt, Tauler, Susa, etc., here directly connected with the only two Dominican devotions, to Mary and to Joseph), but this humanity experienced as a personal manifestation of God's joy for humankind – is the centre of Dominican spirituality and mysticism without any predilection for 'derivative devotions'. All this is typical of the twelfth century; along with all the other characteristics it is also typically Dominican.

4. *Présence au monde (la grâce d'entendre ce siècle,* as Père Lacordaire says): openness for constantly new charismata which different circumstances require of us. Hence the need for structures which do not hem us in but are democratic and flexible, through which it becomes possible for Dominicans to accept the rise of new stories that go against the grain. It is characteristic that the Dominicans never had their Constitutions approved by the pope, so that they themselves could adapt them to new circumstances

5. (As a consequence of 4.): Since Albert and Thomas, Dominican spirituality has been inwardly enriched by the inclusion of the Christian principle of secularization within the essentially religious, gospel trend (Dominicans at first rejected this, but soon they generally accepted it). This involves first coming to know things (objects, inter-personal relationships, society) in their intrinsic characteristics and their own structures rather than prematurely defining their relationship to God. In modern times this has enormous consequences by comparison with all kinds of forms of pseudo-mystical supernaturalism, which often ends up as a sense of superiority masquerading as piety.

To begin with, the Order agonized over the introduction of 'natural sources' into Dominican evangelism. The traditional rejection of the 'profane sciences' by the monks continued to have an effect, though this was limited by the Dominican principle of dispensation. The first Dominicans were 'anti-philosophical' (thus running the risk of an evangelical supernaturalism). The *Vitae Fratrum* reeked of 'holy naivety'. Albert and Thomas changed the direction, Albert even arguing fiercely against fellow-brethren 'who thus again want to become the murderers of Socrates'. The dispute was over the consequences of integral evangelism, which Albert and Thomas wanted to be enlightened in character, not naive. In the Chapter of Valenciennes (1259), the trend supported by Albert and Thomas won through: the study of the 'profane sciences' became compulsory in Dominican training.

6. The other elements: a liturgical choral office, monastic observances and community life, are traditional and generally religious, and in this sense not typically Dominican. That was the dangerous recollection of the monastic and canonical past to which Dominic continued to give expression in his new religious and apostolic programme, albeit in critical, reduced and more modest form.

7. The 'principle of dispensation' (historically this seems to go back to Dominic himself in person), i.e. respect for the particular personal charisma of a fellow Dominican within the Dominican community, bearing in mind the purpose of the Order. Of course this is an extremely dangerous principle, which has been abused to disastrous effect. However, Dominic would rather take that risk than give up the human and Christian significance of the dispensation principle because of the threat of abuse. As a general principle this was a completely new Dominican discovery in the Middle Ages. In furtherance of study in the service of the 'salvation of men' *(salus animarum)* and in furtherance of the apostolate, it is, paradoxically, possible to be a Dominican (if necessary) on your own. This presupposes having been trained as a Dominican, but it is in no way understood as a matter of standing outside the law: on the contrary, dispensation is a constitutional Dominican law. Conformity is alien to the original Dominican legislation. Even now, this original Dominican principle opens up broad possibilities for 'modern experiments' in our time, even experiments which some people accustomed to an 'established' Dominican spirituality cannot stand. (However, these experiments also always need to happen from and within the dangerous recollection of a tradition which is already centuries old. This tradition prefigures permanent perspec-

tives which are always worth thinking about – without it all experiments seem doomed to religious failure.)

Although there are countless examples of this characteristic from our rich family archives, I want to point to just one event in the first redactions of our Dominican Constitutions. (The striking 'democratic structure' of our Order has been said by experts in administration to be unique among Catholic monastic institutions.) This feature can be understood precisely as a result of the typical cross-grained spirituality of the Order (along with its respect for all that is good in the tradition). The Constitutions were 'reformulated' during a revision at a time when great canon lawyers from the universities of the time had entered the Order (for example, Raymond of Penafort). This reformulation took place at a General Chapter in Bologna. Shortly before and during this Chapter, social protests were voiced in the university and city of Bologna, and in addition there was already a dispute between the Ghibellines (the conservatives) and the Guelphs (the progressive popular party). Dominicans were involved throughout this conflict as advisors. The 'co-responsibility of all' required by the progressive party had its influence on our Dominican Constitutions. ('What affects all must also be resolved on by all.') This new civic principle called for at that time was also supported by the Dominicans and later sanctioned in our Dominican Constitutions (under the influence and as a result of the civic experiences in Bologna). New 'secular experiences' thus came to exercise a substantial influence on our earliest Constitutions. The emancipatory social movements of that time left a substantial mark on our Constitutions, differing completely from the traditional administrative model then current. Following the example of Dominic, these Dominicans did not just raise a warning finger and point to what had been the custom from earliest times, but at the same time listened to the voice of God in what came out of the human secular emancipatory movements of the time (however turbulently). As a result of these experiences they rewrote the Dominican monastic structure, barely twenty years after Dominic. That is just one case of the cross-thread that the Dominican family story keeps showing as its 'own theme' down the ages.

I have recalled only a few Dominican characteristics: more could be mentioned. Furthermore, I should point out explicitly that I am in (no way denying that perhaps non-Dominicans do the same things.) In that case Dominican spirituality can simply say with delight: all the better! It is not our concern to maintain an unparalleled exclusiveness. It is a question of what we, as Dominicans, do here in any case, and do in the strength of the charisma of the Order and our Dominican commitment (through our profession). If others also do the same thing, this can simply confirm the validity, the correct intuition of our view. (When a typical view is universalized, it in no way loses its value: quite the opposite.)

The man who was once an Augustinian canon, Domingo de Guzmán, while trusting in the original direction of his life, nevertheless gave it a new course (which became the beginning of the Dominican Order), thanks to a living contact with needs of people and of the church of which he was unaware when he was first called. One cannot accuse Dominic of betraying his first calling, which was meant to be irrevocable. His change of course was a new way of life (in contact with what then appeared to him to be better possibilities), in order to remain faithful to the deepest sense of his calling, when confronted with new needs. (According to Dominic's earliest biographers he could be moved to tears at the sight of the needs of others. Hence the desire of this realistic organizer – which remained with him all his life - to go to the Cumani, somewhere in the Balkans, evidently the place where the dualistic heresy crossed from East to West.) The Order came into being from such an amazing change of course in trust. A change of course in trust is therefore part of the essence of the Dominican charisma.

No theologian, canon lawyer, professional psychologist or sociologist can work out at his study desk or in his armchair what we must do now. This must be tried by way of concrete experiment, by charismatically inspired religious, albeit bearing in mind the sometimes dangerously cross-grained element – the golden thread – in our Dominican family story. In so doing it will adopt, with due criticism, the successful attempts in the context of our past, gratefully rethinking them and making them fruitful in the context of the new programme. With Thomas Aquinas, who clearly followed the matter-of-fact and brilliant temperament of Dominic here, we can say, 'The excellence of a religious institution does not lie so much in the strictness of its observances as in the fact that these observances are designed with greater skill towards the purpose of the religious life.' And in the circumstances of our time this calls for a renewed and skilled religious decision in which all have a share, both high and low, so that the structures themselves remain open to this new cross-thread.)

This question is our duty. For in our profession we also opt for a particular community, a Dominican community and its ideals. There can be such faults and defects in a particular community (whether through betrayal of the Dominican family story or because this story is no longer alive there and has become fossilized and dead) that *out of faithfulness* to his or her Dominican ideal the professed religious is ethically permitted (and in some cases may even be obliged) to leave the Dominican community because it does not give him or her the support to which they have a right by virtue of their profession. For paradoxically, here we expose ourselves to the danger that as Dominicans we may expel a 'Dominican charisma' from our ranks. The Dominican family story gives us adequate pointers if we also listen to God's voice in the characteristics of contemporary movements and trace their lines of force, so as to enrich this story with a new chapter which is still to be published. Many people think that the Dominican family story is exhausted, because hardly anyone still comes under its spell. Those of us who are Dominicans today, men and women, are the only ones who can give it a new twist so that the story flourishes again (not as a stunt or a sensation but as an authentic Dominican family story), so that others in turn will join the Dominican story-telling community and continue to hand the story on. Here we may also happily pass on the folklore which each order has alongside its own great story: that simply points to the fact that the great Dominican family story is made up of, and told by, ordinary, very human, people, though they transcend themselves through the strength of God's unmerited and loving grace. However, it would be fatal for the Dominican family story if this greater story eventually became narrower and was reduced to the story of the folklore of Dominican houses.

I am aware that I have said a great deal and very little. That is perhaps the most appropriate thing for the chapter which we are all adding, here and now, to the story of a great family tradition. I hope that it will become a serial which lasts longer than the stories which have entranced the whole world on television, but which have not in any way renewed the face of the earth: Neighbours, Coronation Street or the Forsyte Saga. May the Dominican story be a parable which in an unspoken, but compelling, way ends with the words of Jesus: 'Go and do likewise' (Luke 10.37).

In 1206, even before Dominic was thinking of a Dominican Order, he had founded a convent at Prouille. However, the aim of this convent was on the same lines: Dominic wanted to make the evangelical religious movement, which many women had also joined, into a church movement – that is,(to bring the gospel to the church and to bring the church to sectarian gospel movements.) Evangelism without the church or the church without evangelism is essentially un-Dominican, that is, it goes against the original charisma which brought the Order into being.

In Dominic's time, gospel inspiration was almost always to be found in 'deviant' movements. Hence Dominic's own preaching among the 'heretics'. From among such women (Waldensians who remained orthodox, the 'Catholic Poor') Dominic recruited the first occupants of Prouille:(he gave a church atmosphere to the gospel they had experienced outside the church.)In 1219 he also founded convents in Madrid and Rome (S. Sisto), to which he gave Constitutions (which would later also form the basis of the Dominican Order). After many difficulties the convent of S. Agnese was founded at Bologna with the financial support of an 18-year-old girl, Diana of Andalo (later the friend of the second General, Jordan of Saxony), but only after Dominic's death.

However, it is typical that at the end of his life Dominic, and after his death the whole male side of the Order, systematically began to oppose the incorporation of new convents into the Order. This opposition would involve them in fights with popes until 1259. It is evident from the archives that this opposition was motivated by the aim of the Order itself: (the care of the sisters hindered the Dominicans in their task of preaching elsewhere.) At a special Chapter in 1228 (in Paris) all Dominicans were prohibited from involvement in spiritual direction and pastoral care in our convents (with the exception of the first four great convents), on pain of expulsion from the Order. In northern areas, however, the growing Dominican movement had encountered the very lively evangelical women's movement there: all of a sudden this became Dominican (or sometimes Franciscan). After a time there were hundreds of convents, each with more than a hundred evangelical Dominican women. (No one had planned this: it was a spontaneous consequence of the encounter between Dominican preaching and the evangelical women's movement of the time) After that, the male Dominicans came to be fundamentally opposed to having to care for the sisters, which hindered the purpose of their own Order. Time and again, papal bulls enjoined the Order against its will to provide both financial and spiritual care for these sisters. In 1252, at the Chapter of Bologna, the Order opposed the repeated papal bulls (occasioned by an appeal from our sisters to Rome). In a bull of 15 July 1252, Innocent IV made some concessions: Rome would stop issuing the bulls for the moment but the existing convents had to be taken into the care of the Dominicans. However, the Dominicans would not accept this, and in the end they secured a retraction from the same pope, who said: 'I have allowed myself to be convinced that preaching is the most essential task of the Order) This aim must have priority and is hindered by the care of the women's convents. Therefore the pope resolves to release the Order from all obligations towards the convents ... with the exceptions of Prouille and San Sisto in Rome.'

However, all the convents stormed the papal Curia with heartfelt pleas. The pope was caught between two Dominican fronts: the men and the women. He knew that the men were opposed in principle. Then the Master General, Jobannes Teutonicus, died (in 1252). Cardinal Hugo a Santo Caro, who had become a Dominican and was himself enthusiastic about the evangelical women's movement, was given full authority by the pope to come to an arrangement with the Order. First he wanted to break the opposition of the men 'with quiet measures': until the election of the new General (Humbert of Romans), the Dominicans had at least to take over the spiritual care of the sisters. The Order remained obstinate and at the Chapter of Milan in 1255 it was resolved that (in contrast to the monasteries) three successive General Chapters would be needed to come to a decision as to whether a convent was to come under Dominican direction. This first resolution was endorsed in Paris (1256) and Florence (1257) and thus became a Dominican ruling. In 1259 a definitive resolution was passed that all convents already established had the right to the pastoral care of Dominican priests. (This ending of resistance by the Order was the result of the mediation of the Dominican cardinal Hugo a Santo Caro, who combined both the official Dominican standpoint and that of the church in his own person. In the Order, from Dominic onwards, the specific Dominican character was often a compromise between the papal perspective and the views of the Dominicans; both parties knew how to secure the essentials of their position.) (After about 30 years of opposition the Order capitulated: for new convents, the Dominican resolution, passed by three Chapters, remained in force. The combination of papal Curia and Dominican sisters had won the argument.) Furthermore, the Order was obliged to make Constitutions for the whole of the women's side. In the General Chapter of 1259 at Valenciennes, Humbert of Romans approved the Dominican Constitutions as adapted for sisters. All this also gave the sisters economic security, so that they could devote themselves to a life of study and contemplation (since left to themselves, the sisters often lived in very real poverty – as a result of over-population). The close collaboration of male and female Dominicans that now took place resulted in the Dominican mystical movement which arose in the fourteenth century. This followed from the theological and mystical direction of women by Dominican lectors and the women's response to the direction (1300-1480). This was in the time of the Great Plague, which also affected thousands of Dominicans and had broken their initial verve. Furthermore, the Order was divided by the schism: Avignon and the two popes.

Later, above all in the nineteenth century, many congregations of sisters were founded outside the Order, so that the Order did not have any responsibility for them and no one was concerned for a truly Dominican spirituality: this spirit was often that of normal nineteenth-century religious life with its inspiration towards works of charity.

As Dominicans, therefore, (we need to remember that in our day many developments have taken place in which men and women together are seeking a form of Dominican spirituality in a modern revival of life in accordance with the gospel, combined with social criticism.) Although it is still a search, we may not simply rule out this Dominican possibility. A Dominican community spirit and the collaboration of Dominican brothers and sisters may perhaps help us to understand the mystical Dominican movement in the fourteenth century (a high point of Dominican spirituality). Taught by our own history, we may not dismiss possible new charismata out of hand. 'Dominican options' which are new and at first sight disconcerting are possibilities for the future and may not be suppressed *per se,* though we must pay attention to the danger of references to the religious past.

Bibliography

It did not seem appropriate to provide a short book like this with an extensive set of notes. Nevertheless I want to justify my view of Dominican spirituality and provide readers with the sources of the information that I give here; and I do not want to send away empty-handed those who want to read more in connection with a particular section. So here, chapter by chapter, is information about the literature I have used and books which readers may want to consult.

Introduction

H.-D. Lacordaire lived from 1802 to 1861. His *Mémoire pour le rétablissement en France de l'Ordre de Frères Prêcheurs* appeared in 1839 and his *Vie de St Dominique* in 1841. There is an English translation of the *Mémoire* edited by Simon Tugwell in *Dominican Sources* 2, Oak Park, Illinois and Dublin 1983. There is an account of Lacordaire's life by L. C. Sheppard, London and New York 1964.

Michael Hensen wrote his book in 1947. He was influenced by the discussion about Dominican life in France and especially by Lacordaire. He was later to leave the Dominican Order and as Wilfried Hensen became a Remonstrant preacher and wrote a number of books on spirituality.

Chapter 1

The view of religious life presented here ultimately goes back to the view of Johann Baptist Metz and the German Dominican Tiemo Reiner Peters.

For the Rule of Augustine of Hippo see G. P. Lawless, OSA,

Augustine of Hippo and his Monastic Rule, Oxford 1987, which has the text in Latin and English and a commentary; there is a text and English translation of the Rule of Benedict by J. McCann, OSB, London 1952.

Dirc van Delf was born around 1365 and there are no traces of him after 1404. The historical judgment on the mendicant orders quoted here comes from R. H. Coats, 'Holiness: New Testament and Christian' in the classical *Encyclopaedia of Religion and Ethics* 6, Edinburgh 1913, pp. 743-50: 747.

For the interest and significance of the veneration of Mary Magdalene in the mendicant orders, especially the Dominicans, see K. L. Jansen, *The Making of the Magdalen. Preaching and Popular Devotion in the Later Middle Ages*, Princeton 2000. The largely hidden history of women in the first decades of the Dominican movement has been reconstructed in J. A. K McNamara, *Sisters in Arms. Catholic Nuns through Two Millennia*, Cambridge, Mass. and London 1996, pp. 312-17. For the custom of branding as prostitutes women who preached cf. B. M. Kienzle, 'The Prostitute-Preacher: Patterns of Polemic against Mediaeval Waldensian Women Preachers' in B. M. Kienzle and P. J. Walker (eds), *Women Preachers and Prophets through Two Millennia of Christianity*, Berkeley, Los Angeles and London 1998, pp. 99-113. There is an interesting article in this collection on the role of women in the Cathar church: A. Brianon, 'The Voice of the Good Women. An Essay on the Pastoral and Sacerdotal Role of Women in the Cathar Church' (pp. 114-33). And Katherine Ludwig gives a summary of her study of the image of Mary Magdalene listed above (pp. 57-96).

The story of Thecla can be found as part of 'The Acts of Paul' in E. Hennecke, W. Schneemelcher and R. McL. Wilson, *New Testament Apocrypha* 2, Louisville and Cambridge 1992, pp. 239-46.

Chapter 2

There are of course many biographies of Dominic. There is a fine illustrated account by Simon Tugwell, at present head of the Dominican historical institute. Tugwell sets out his view of the history of the life of Dominic at length in a series of long 'Notes on the Life of Saint Dominic' in *Archivum Fratrum Praedicatorum*, the historical journal of the Dominicans (65, 1995, pp. 50-169; 66, 1996, pp. 5-200; 67, 1997, pp. 27-59). Among other things he concludes that there is no hard historical evidence that Dominic indeed came from the Guzmán family. For Dominic's life and views and for the text of the earliest sources see V. Koudelka, *Dominic*, London 1997.

That preaching is the central element of Dominican spirituality and that this governs the bold treatment by Dominicans of the tradition of the religious life is the central thesis of Simon Tugwell's book *The Way of the Preacher*, London 1979, and has been further supported in his edition of texts of early Dominican history, *Early Dominicans*, in the series The Classics of Western Spirituality. A Library of the Great Spiritual Masters, London 1981; most documents referred to here can be found there in translation. The idea that the Dominican orientation on preaching implies a specific view of God and God's relation to the world has been derived from a long duplicated article that Edward Schillebeeckx produced in 1954 to introduce Flemish Dominican theological students to Dominican spirituality. Despite plans for publication, this never appeared; cf. the first volume of my biography of Edward Schillebeeckx, which will be published in English in 2002. In an article included as a postscript to this book, Schillebeeckx develops the well-known notion that Dominic brought into the church discoveries of currents which were later regarded as heretical, combined with the view that Dominican spirituality tends to go against the grain

M. H. Vicaire investigates the history of the idea of an apostolic life in his *L'initiation des apôtres: Moines, chanoines, mendiants (IVe-XIIIe siècles)*, Paris 1963. The complicated position and the ambiguous history of Dominican laity within what developed as a priestly order becomes clear in Vicaire's article 'Les origines paradoxales du Tiers-Ordre de Saint Dominique' in his book *Dominique et ses Prêcheurs*, Fribourg and Paris 1977, pp. 392-409. When from the 1930s on the insight grew that the church does not stand over against the world but preaches God's presence in the midst of the world, the Dominican theologian and historian Marie-Dominique Chenu was led to describe the Dominican movement as part of the broad spiritual reform movement of the twelfth and thirteenth centuries which was above all supported by the laity. Cf. M.-D. Chenu, *La parole de Dieu II, L'évangile dans le temps*, Paris 1964: see pp. 37-53, 'Réformes de structures en chrétienté' (1946); pp. 55-69; 'L'experience des spirituels au XIIIe siècle' (1953); and pp. 71-83, 'Laics en chrétienté' (1945). Chenu also demonstrated in 'Moines, clercs, laïcs au carrefour de la Vie Evangelique (XIIe siècle)', *Revue d'historie ecclésiastique* 49, 1954, pp. 59ff., that a new picture of the relationship between God and the world also developed in this movement.

There is a survey of the state of research into the Cathar movement in M. Lambert, *The Cathars*, Oxford 1998. The paraphrased sentences from Ben Okri come from his collection of essays *A Way of Being Free*, London 1998.

Chapter 3

The quotation from Assia Djebar comes from *Vast is the Prison*, New York 1995. The poem by J. Hyvrard comes from her collection *La meurtritude*, Paris 1977. The poem by Vera Huigen from which I quote, entitled 'People of the Way', appears in *Tot zover deze lezing. De zondagse lezingen van het B-jaar gelezen door vrouwen*, Baarn 1996, p. 35. That suffering can produce the experience of the absence of the good and so in a paradoxical way become the space for the divine presence is worked out by Edward Schillebeeckx under the term 'contrast experience'; cf. his *Christ*, London and New York 1980.

Alexandro Jodorowsky's book was first published in Spanish in 1992. That for Thomas Aquinas God is not an object alongside others but can be known by those who perceive reality in a particular way is most clearly evident in *Summa theologiae I*, Quaestio 1, articulus 3.

The conversation between Peter and Mary Magdalene is in the 'Gospel according to Mary' (Magdalene) which probably comes from the second or third century. There is a translation and discussion of the book by Esther de Boer, *Mary Magdalene. Beyond the Myth*, London and Harrisburg, Pa. 1997. See also G. L. King in *Searching the Scriptures II: A Feminist Commentary*, ed. E. Schüssler Fiorenza, New York and London 1994, pp. 601-34. For the title *apostola apostolorum* for Mary Magdalene see S. Haskins, *Mary Magdalen. Myth and Metaphor*, London 1993, ch. 3.

Schillebeeckx worked out that God in the Dominican sense is first and foremost a *Deus salutaris* in his 1954 duplicated article, mentioned in connection with the previous chapter. For the importance of compassion for a Christian spirituality in the midst of present-day society, see the book by the former Dominican M. Fox, *A Spirituality named Compassion and the Healing of the Global Village, Humpty Dumpty and Us*, Minneapolis 1979.

There is an accessible English translation by S. Noffke of Catherine's most important writing, *The Dialogue on Divine Providence*, in the series Classics of Western Spirituality, *The Dialogue*, London 1970. For further investigation of her life and work and its possible current significance cf. S. Noffke, *Catherine of Siena. Vision through a Distant Eye*, Collegeville 1996.

Eckhart talks in the sermon *Populus eius in te est, misereberis* of God's mercy, which I here translate compassion; this is of the nature of God and must be born in the soul. The German text can be found in J. Quint (ed.), *Meister Eckehart. Deutsche Predigten und Traktate*, Munich 1963, pp. 188-90. The distinction that Thomas Aquinas makes between the various religious activities, along with the sentence *maius est contemplata aliis tradere quam solum contemplari* can be found in his *Summa theologiae* IIa IIae, Quaestio 188, articulus 6.

Timothy Radcliffe speaks of 'the freedom to belong' as opposed to 'the freedom to escape', which he regards as the flight for our own deepest nature', in 'Jurassic Park and the Last Supper', which is included in a readable collection of texts from his period as Master of the Dominican order, *Sing a New Song. The Christian Vocation*, Dublin 1999. The sentence 'In a broken time with cynicism as God, this is possibly a heresy', comes from Ben Okri's *A Way of Being Free*, mentioned earlier.

Chapter 4

The quotation from Judy Petsonk comes from the introductory chapter to her book *Taking Judaism Personally. Creating a Meaningful Spiritual Life*, New York 1996, pp. 3-7, entitled 'Entering the Gate: In Which I Find God in a Pile of Laundry. Which Sounds Like a Comedown from Sinai. But Isn't.'

There is an English translation of the second part of Humbert of Romans' treatise on the formation of preachers in Tugwell's *Early Dominicans*, mentioned in connection with chapter 2. The reference to Bernard of Clairvaux is on pp. 234-5. The objections referred to come from Tugwell's *The Way of the Preacher*, also mentioned in chapter 2.

For *The Nine Ways of Prayer of St Dominic* I have based myself on the text in Tugwell's *Early Dominicans*. There are several translations of the *Spiritual Exercises* of Ignatius of Loyola. The most accessible is that by A. Mottola, New York 1978. The anecdote about Thomas Aquinas praying can be found in M. Carruthers, *The Book of Memory. The Study of Memory in Mediaeval Culture*, London 1990, p. 202. The Christian view of the psalms as the inner voice of the biblical writings, Old and New Testament, was expressed in a very clear and committed way by Martin Luther in his preface to the Psalter, the preface to the book of Psalms in his own translation.

There has been a long discussion of the Dominican experience of poverty, with the accepted outcome that in contrast to the Franciscans, Dominicans do not regard poverty as representing any mystical value – cf. Francis' poem about Lady Poverty – but it must not be seen as simply a strategy for making preaching credible. (It is even a form of preaching.) Lacordaire already made this point in general terms in his famous *Mémoire* mentioned in the introduction to this book.

In this book I cannot go into the history of the Inquisition in general and within it also that of the persecution of witches and the role of the Dominicans in this, which was considerable. For a history of the Inquisition set within a wider social and political context see B. F. Hamilton, *The Medieval Inquisition,* London 1981.

Chapter 5

Bruce Chatwin sets out the basic view of his *Anatomy of Restlessness, Uncollected Writings*, London 1997, above all in Part III of the book, on 'The Nomadic Alternative'.

The facts about Antonio de Montesinos, Bartolomé de Las Casas and the history of the period can be found in G. Gutierrez, *Las Casas in Search of the Poor of Jesus Christ,* Maryknoll, NY 1994. E. Galeano writes about de Montesinos' activities in *Memory of Fire*, Part I, 'The Beginning', London 1995. P. Neruda's poem about Las Casas is in *Canto General*, Amsterdam 1986, pp. 104-6. Etty Hillesum called herself 'the thinking heart of the barracks' in a letter from the Westerbork transit camp. See Etty Hillesum, *An Interrupted Life; The Diaries of Etty Hillesum 1941-1943*, London and New York 1984.

Postscript

The text by Timothy Radcliffe to which I refer is included in his collection *Sing a New Song*, mentioned in connection with chapter 3, under the title 'Religious Vocation. Leaving Behind the Usual Signs of Identity' (pp. 191–209).